Pakistan's Nuclear Weapons: Proliferation and Security Issues

Paul K. Kerr
Analyst in Nonproliferation

Mary Beth Nikitin
Specialist in Nonproliferation

June 26, 2012

Congressional Research Service

7-5700

www.crs.gov

RL34248

CRS Report for Congress ─────────────────

Prepared for Members and Committees of Congress

Summary

Pakistan's nuclear arsenal probably consists of approximately 90-110 nuclear warheads, although it could be larger. Islamabad is producing fissile material, adding to related production facilities, and deploying additional delivery vehicles. These steps could enable Pakistan to undertake both quantitative and qualitative improvements to its nuclear arsenal. Whether and to what extent Pakistan's current expansion of its nuclear weapons-related facilities is a response to the 2008 U.S.-India nuclear cooperation agreement is unclear. Islamabad does not have a public, detailed nuclear doctrine, but its "minimum credible deterrent" is widely regarded as designed to dissuade India from taking military action against Pakistan.

Pakistan has in recent years taken a number of steps to increase international confidence in the security of its nuclear arsenal. In addition to overhauling nuclear command and control structures since September 11, 2001, Islamabad has implemented new personnel security programs. Moreover, Pakistani and some U.S. officials argue that, since the 2004 revelations about a procurement network run by former Pakistani nuclear official A. Q. Khan, Islamabad has taken a number of steps to improve its nuclear security and to prevent further proliferation of nuclear-related technologies and materials. A number of important initiatives, such as strengthened export control laws, improved personnel security, and international nuclear security cooperation programs have improved Pakistan's security situation in recent years.

However, instability in Pakistan has called the extent and durability of these reforms into question. Some observers fear radical takeover of a government that possesses a nuclear bomb, or proliferation by radical sympathizers within Pakistan's nuclear complex in case of a breakdown of controls. While U.S. and Pakistani officials continue to express confidence in controls over Pakistan's nuclear weapons, continued instability in the country could impact these safeguards. For a broader discussion, see CRS Report RL33498, *Pakistan-U.S. Relations*, by K. Alan Kronstadt. This report will be updated.

This report updates a previous version published November 30, 2011.

Contents

Contacts

Background

Chronic political instability in Pakistan and Islamabad's military efforts against the Taliban and al-Qaeda have raised concerns about the security of Pakistan's nuclear weapons. Some observers fear that Pakistan's strategic nuclear assets could be obtained by terrorists or used by elements in the Pakistani government. Chairman of the Joint Chiefs of Staff Admiral Michael Mullen described U.S. concern about the matter during a September 22, 2008, speech:

> To the best of my ability to understand it—and that is with some ability—the weapons there are secure. And that even in the change of government, the controls of those weapons haven't changed. That said, they are their weapons. They're not my weapons. And there are limits to what I know. Certainly at a worst-case scenario with respect to Pakistan, I worry a great deal about those weapons falling into the hands of terrorists and either being proliferated or potentially used. And so, control of those, stability, stable control of those weapons is a key concern. And I think certainly the Pakistani leadership that I've spoken with on both the military and civilian side understand that.

U.S. officials have generally expressed confidence in the security of Pakistan's nuclear weapons. President Obama addressed this issue in an April 29, 2009, press conference, stating, "I'm confident that we can make sure that Pakistan's nuclear arsenal is secure, primarily, initially, because the Pakistani army, I think, recognizes the hazards of those weapons falling into the wrong hands. We've got strong military-to-military consultation and cooperation." He also recognized the sensitivity of the issue for Pakistan, saying, "[w]e want to respect their sovereignty, but we also recognize that we have huge strategic interests, huge national security interests in making sure that Pakistan is stable and that you don't end up having a nuclear-armed militant state."[1] Declining to engage in "hypotheticals" when asked if the United States is ready to secure the nuclear arsenal if the Pakistani government could not do so, President Obama said he felt "confident that that nuclear arsenal will remain out of militant hands." More recently, Department of State spokesperson Mark Toner told reporters May 26, 2011, that "the safeguard and security of Pakistan's nuclear weapons are of concern, but ... it's an issue that we discussed with the Pakistani government, and we're sure that they're under safeguard." Toner also stated November 9, 2011, that the United States "continue[s] to have confidence in the government of Pakistan that they both understand the threat to their nuclear arsenal, the varied threats to their nuclear arsenal, that they're taking appropriate steps to safeguard them."

U.S. intelligence officials have articulated similar assessments. Then-Director of National Intelligence Dennis Blair told the House Permanent Select Committee on Intelligence February 3, 2010, that "from what we see of ... measures that they take," Pakistan is keeping its nuclear weapons secure. Lieutenant General Burgess, Director of the Defense Intelligence Agency, stated in March 10, 2011, testimony before the Senate Armed Services Committee that "Pakistan is able to safeguard its nuclear weapons, including protecting important segments of its nuclear program in underground facilities," but added that "vulnerabilities still exist."[2]

---

[1] President Obama's 100th-Day Press Briefing transcript, April 29, 2009, accessed at http://www nytimes.com/2009/04/29/us/politics/29text-obama html?_r=1&pagewanted=print.

[2] Ronald L. Burgess, Jr. Lieutenant General, U.S. Army Director, Defense Intelligence Agency, World Wide Threat Assessment: Statement before the Committee on Armed Services, United States Senate," March 10, 2011, available at http://www.dia mil/public-affairs/testimonies/2011-03-10 html.

The collapse or near-collapse of the Pakistani government is probably the most likely scenario in which militants or terrorists could acquire Pakistani nuclear weapons. General David H. Petraeus, the former Commander of U.S. Central Command, testified March 31, 2009, that "Pakistani state failure would provide transnational terrorist groups and other extremist organizations an opportunity to acquire nuclear weapons and a safe haven from which to plan and launch attacks." More recently, Gary Samore, National Security Council Coordinator for Arms Control and Non-Proliferation, stated in an April 2011 interview that

> The Pakistani government takes the nuclear security threat very seriously, and they've put a lot of resources into trying to make sure that their nuclear facilities and materials and weapons are well secured. There's no lack of recognition that this is a very important issue, and there's no lack of incentive on the part of the Pakistani government to maintain control. What I worry about is that, in the context of broader tensions and problems within Pakistani society and polity—and that's obviously taking place as we look at the sectarian violence and tensions between the government and the military and so forth—I worry that, in that broader context, even the best nuclear security measures might break down. You're dealing with a country that is under tremendous stress internally and externally, and that's what makes me worry. They have good programs in place; the question is whether those good programs work in the context where these broader tensions and conflicts are present.[3]

Additionally, former Pakistani President Pervez Musharraf told CNN May 26, 2011, that "[i]f Pakistan disintegrates, then it can be dangerous. Otherwise, if Pakistan's integrity is there, and which I'm sure it will be there as long as the armed forces of Pakistan are there, there is no danger of the nuclear assets or strategic assets falling in any terrorist hands."[4]

Pakistani efforts to improve the security of its nuclear weapons have been ongoing and include some cooperation with the United States; Musharraf told a journalist that Islamabad has "given State Department nonproliferation experts insight into the command and control of the Pakistani arsenal and its on-site safety and security procedures."[5] Since the 1998 Pakistani and Indian nuclear tests, the international community has increased attention to reducing the risk of nuclear war in South Asia. The two countries most recently came to the brink of full-scale war in 1999 and 2002, and, realizing the dangers, have developed some risk reduction measures to prevent accidental nuclear war. Islamabad has also developed its command and control systems and improved the security of its military and civilian nuclear facilities. Since the 2004 revelations of an extensive international nuclear proliferation network run by Pakistani nuclear official Abdul Qadeer Khan, as well as possible connections between Pakistani nuclear scientists and Al Qaeda, Islamabad has made additional efforts to improve export controls and monitor nuclear personnel. The main security challenges for Pakistan's nuclear arsenal are keeping the integrity of the command structure, ensuring physical security, and preventing illicit proliferation from insiders.

Pakistan continues to produce fissile material for weapons and appears to be augmenting its weapons production facilities, as well as deploying additional delivery vehicles—steps that will enable both quantitative and qualitative improvements in Islamabad's nuclear arsenal.

---

[3] Peter Crail, Daniel Horner, and Daryl G. Kimball, "Pursuing the Prague Agenda: An Interview With White House Coordinator Gary Samore," *Arms Control Today*, May 2011.

[4] "Interview with Pervez Musharraf," *Piers Morgan Tonight*, CNN, May 26, 2011.

[5] Seymour M. Hersh, "Defending the Arsenal: In an Unstable Pakistan, Can Nuclear Warheads be Kept Safe?" *The New Yorker*, November 16, 2009.

Nuclear Weapons[6]

Pakistan's nuclear energy program dates back to the 1950s, but it was the loss of East Pakistan (now Bangladesh) in a war with India that probably triggered a January 1972 political decision (just one month later) to begin a secret nuclear weapons program.[7] Deterring India's nuclear weapons and augmenting Pakistan's inferior conventional forces are widely believed to be the primary missions for Islamabad's nuclear arsenal. Observers point to India's 1974 "peaceful" nuclear explosion as the pivotal moment that gave additional urgency to the program. Pakistan produced fissile material for its nuclear weapons using gas-centrifuge-based uranium enrichment technology, which it mastered by the mid-1980s. Highly-enriched uranium (HEU) is one of two types of fissile material used in nuclear weapons; the other is plutonium. The country's main enrichment facility is a centrifuge plant located at Kahuta; Pakistan may have other enrichment sites.[8] Islamabad gained enrichment-related technology from many sources. This extensive assistance is reported to have included uranium enrichment technology from Europe, blueprints for a small nuclear weapon from China, and missile technology from China.

The United States had information during the 1970s that Pakistan was constructing a uranium enrichment facility.[9] A. Q. Khan has stated that Pakistan began enriching uranium in 1978 and produced HEU in 1983.[10] [11]Although Pakistan subsequently told the United States that it would produce only low-enriched uranium (which is not used as fissile material in nuclear weapons),[12] U.S. and Pakistani officials who were in government in 1990 indicated during a 1994 meeting that Islamabad decided sometime after October 1989 to resume producing HEU.[13] However,

---

[6] Pakistan has signed neither the nuclear Nonproliferation Treaty nor the Comprehensive Test Ban Treaty. However, UN Security Council Resolution 1172, which was adopted in 1998 after India and Pakistan's nuclear tests earlier that year, called upon those countries to "stop their nuclear weapon development programmes, to refrain from weaponization or from the deployment of nuclear weapons, to cease development of ballistic missiles capable of delivering nuclear weapons and any further production of fissile material for nuclear weapons."

[7] See, for example, U.S. Department of Defense, *Proliferation: Threat and Response,* April 1996, p. 37.

[8] Zia Mian, A.H. Nayyar, R. Rajaraman and M.V. Ramana, "Fissile Materials in South Asia: The Implications of the U.S.-India Nuclear Deal," International Panel on Fissile Materials, September 2006 and David Albright, "Securing Pakistan's Nuclear Infrastructure," in *A New Equation: U.S. Policy toward India and Pakistan after September 11* (Washington: Carnegie Endowment for International Peace) May 2002. For a list of Pakistani nuclear facilities, see chart in Pakistan chapter of Joseph Cirincione, Jon B. Wolfsthal, and Miriam Rajkumar, *Deadly Arsenals,* Carnegie Endowment for International Peace, 2005.

[9] For example, a 1978 memorandum from the National Intelligence Officer for Nuclear Proliferation stated that Pakistan had a uranium enrichment plant "under construction," but added that Islamabad had not yet acquired certain key components. Available at http://www.gwu.edu/~nsarchiv/nukevault/ebb333/doc03.pdf.

[10] "Nuclear Bomb Was Manufactured in 1984: Dr Abdul Qadir Khan," *Islamabad Jinnah,* July 19, 2010; "Pakistan: Dr Abdul Qadeer Khan Discusses Nuclear Program in TV Talk Show," Islamabad Tonight, *Aaj News Television,* August 31, 2009.

[11] Two non-Pakistani sources appear to at least partly corroborate this account. First, a 1981 State Department draft paper indicated that Pakistan had not "proceeded to the systematic separation of special nuclear materials, or the assembly and deployment of nuclear weapons." (Special Assistant for Nuclear Proliferation Intelligence, National Foreign Assessment Center, Central Intelligence Agency, to Resource Management Staff, Office of Program Assessment et al., "Request for Review of Draft Paper on the Security Dimension of Non-Proliferation," April 9, 1981.) Second, according to a 2008 International Atomic Energy Agency report, A.Q. Khan offered centrifuge enrichment technology to Libya in 1984—a data point apparently corroborating the 1983 date. Available at https://iaea.org/Publications/Documents/Board/2008/gov2008-39.pdf.

[12] That agreement is referenced in Shirin Tahir-Kheli, *Memorandum for Robert B. Oakley,* "Dealing with Pakistan's Nuclear Program: A U.S. Strategy." July 23, 1987.

[13] Michael Krepon and Mishi Faruqee, eds., *Conflict Prevention and Confidence-Building Measures in South Asia: The* (continued...)

---

another Pakistani official suggested during the same meeting that the decision may have happened sooner.[14]

The United States had information during the 1970s and early 1980s that Pakistan was pursuing nuclear weapons designs, but exactly when Pakistan produced a workable nuclear explosive device is unclear.[15] A 1985 National Intelligence Council report stated that Pakistan "probably has a workable design for a nuclear explosive device" and was "probably ... a year or two away from a capacity to produce enough" highly enriched uranium for such a device.[16] A 1987 National Security Council (NSC) memorandum described Pakistan's "continued pursuit ... of its nuclear weapons option."[17] A 1993 report to Congress, apparently from the NSC, stated that Islamabad's nuclear weapons efforts "culminated with the capability to rapidly assemble a nuclear device if necessary by the end of the 1980s."[18] A. Q. Khan stated in an interview published in May 1998 that Islamabad "attained" the capability to detonate such a device "at the end of 1984."[19] Similarly, Khan reportedly stated in a January 2010 speech that Pakistan "had become a nuclear power" in 1984 or 1985.[20] Moreover, "senior Pakistani politicians" told a Canadian parliamentary committee in June 1998 that Pakistan had "reached the nuclear 'threshold' by 1984-85," according to a 1998 report.[21] In any case, President Bush's failure to certify in 1990 that Pakistan did not "possess a nuclear explosive device" led to a cut-off in military and financial aid under the Pressler Amendment.[22]

After India conducted nuclear weapon tests on May 11 and May 13, 1998, Pakistan's government responded on May 28 and May 30 with six tests in western Pakistan. Test yields were about 10 kilotons and 5 kilotons, according to seismic analysis.[23] The United States imposed additional

---

(...continued)

1990 Crisis, The Henry L. Stimson Center Occasional Paper No. 17, April 1994, pp. 7, 40, 42.

[14] Krepon and Faruqee, 1994, p. 31.

[15] See, for example, a 1978 Central Intelligence Agency report, available at http://www.faqs.org/cia/docs/44/0000107983/(UNTITLED)-RE.html, as well as a 1983 State Department document, available at http://www.gwu.edu/~nsarchiv/NSAEBB/NSAEBB114/chipak-11.pdf.

[16] According to a 1978 State Department cable, the United States estimated that it would take Pakistan "at least" three to five years to produce a nuclear explosive device. Available at http://www.gwu.edu/~nsarchiv/nukevault/ebb333/doc24.pdf.

[17] Tahir-Kheli, 1987

[18] *Report to Congress on Status of China, India and Pakistan Nuclear and Ballistic Missile Programs*, 1993. Available at http://www.fas.org/irp/threat/930728-wmd htm.

[19] "Pakistan: Qadeer Khan Interviewed on Pakistan N-Test," *The News*, May 30, 1998. Khan made a similar claim in February and July 2010 interviews ("Pakistan: Dr A.Q. Khan Condemns Nawaz Sharif for Not Testing Nuclear Bomb," *Islamabad Khabrain Online*, February 20, 2010; *Islamabad Jinnah*, July 19, 2010).

[20] Khalid Iqbal, "Pakistan to Never Face 1971-Like Situation Again: AQ Khan," *The News*, January 10, 2010.

[21] Bill Graham, M.P, *Canada and the Nuclear Challenge: Reducing the Political Value of Nuclear Weapons for the Twenty-First Century*, Report of the Standing Committee on Foreign Affairs and International Trade, December 1998. Available at http://www.parl.gc.ca/HousePublications/Publication.aspx?DocId=1031537&Language=E&Mode=1&Parl=36&Ses=1.

[22] The Pressler Amendment (August 1985) linked aid and military sales to two certification conditions: (1) that Pakistan not possess a nuclear explosive device; and (2) that new aid 'will reduce significantly the risk' that Pakistan will possess such a device. For background summary of sanctions legislation, see CRS Report 98-486, *Nuclear Sanctions: Section 102(b) of the Arms Export Control Act and Its Application to India and Pakistan*, by Jeanne J. Grimmett, and CRS Report RS22757, *U.S. Arms Sales to Pakistan*, by Richard F. Grimmett.

[23] Seismic data showed yields less than those officially announced by Pakistan and India. See Gregory van der Vink, Jeffrey Park, Richard Allen, Terry Wallace and Christel Hennet, "False Accusations, Undetected Tests and (continued...)

---

sanctions after the tests, but these were lifted after the September 11, 2001, terrorist attacks on the United States. According to public estimates, Pakistan has about 90-110 nuclear weapons, though it could have more.[24] Pakistan's HEU-based nuclear warheads use an implosion design with a solid core of approximately 15-20 kilograms of HEU.[25] Islamabad reportedly continues to produce HEU for weapons at a rate of at least 100 kilograms per year.[26]

Pakistan has also pursued plutonium-based warheads and continues to produce plutonium for weapons.[27] Islamabad has received Chinese and European assistance for at least some of its plutonium program. The 40-50 megawatt heavy-water Khushab plutonium production reactor has been operating since 1998.[28] It appears that Islamabad is constructing three additional heavy-water reactors, which will expand considerably Pakistan's plutonium production capacity, at the same site.[29] Whether one of those reactors is already operating is unclear. Additionally, Pakistan has a reprocessing facility[30] at the Pakistan Institute of Science and Technology (PINSTECH) and is apparently constructing other such facilities. *Nuclear Fuel* reported in 2000 that, according to "senior U.S. government officials," Islamabad had begun operating a "pilot-scale" reprocessing facility at the New Laboratories facility at PINSTECH.[31] Pakistan also appears to be constructing a second reprocessing facility at the site[32] and may be completing a reprocessing facility located

---

(...continued)

Implications for the CTB Treaty," *Arms Control Today*, May 1998. http://www.armscontrol.org/act/1998_05/vimy98.asp.

[24] Karen DeYoung, "New Estimates Put Pakistan's Nuclear Arsenal at More Than 100," *Washington Post*, January 31, 2011; David E. Sanger and Eric Schmitt, "Pakistani Nuclear Arms Pose Challenge to U.S. Policy," *New York Times*, January 31, 2011; Robert Norris and Hans Kristensen, "Nuclear Notebook: Pakistan's Nuclear Forces, 2011," *Bulletin of the Atomic Scientists*, July/August 2011. The International Panel on Fissile Materials estimated in 2008 that Pakistan had enough fissile material (highly enriched uranium and plutonium) for 65-80 nuclear weapons; this estimate assumed 25 kilograms of HEU per weapon and 4.5-6 kilograms of plutonium per weapon ("Banning the Production of Fissile Materials for Nuclear Weapons: Country Perspectives on the Challenges to a Fissile Material (Cutoff) Treaty," International Panel on Fissile Materials, 2008. http://www.fissilematerials.org/ipfm/site_down/gfmr08cv.pdf).

[25] Robert Norris and Hans Kristensen, "Nuclear Notebook: Pakistan's Nuclear Forces, 2007," *Bulletin of the Atomic Scientists*, May/June 2007.

[26] "Global Fissile Material Report 2007," International Panel on Fissile Materials. http://www.fissilematerials.org/ipfm/site_down/gfmr07.pdf.

[27] DIA Director Burgess described Pakistan's nuclear weapons as "based primarily on highly enriched uranium." See Burgess, World Wide Threat Assessment, March 10, 2011.

[28] A Pakistani newspaper reported in April 1998 that, according to a "top government source," the reactor had begun operating ("Pakistan's Indigenous Nuclear Reactor Starts Up," *The Nation*, April 13, 1998). A June 15, 2000 article cited "U.S. officials" who indicated that the reactor had begun operating two years earlier (Mark Hibbs, "After 30 Years, PAEC Fulfills Munir Khan's Plutonium Ambition," *Nucleonics Week*, June 15, 2000). A 2001 Department of Defense report stated that the reactor "will produce plutonium," but did not say whether it was operating (U.S. Department of Defense, *Proliferation: Threat and Response*, January 2001, p. 27).

[29] David Albright and Paul Brannan, "Update on Khushab Plutonium Production Reactor Construction Projects in Pakistan," Institute for Science and International Security, April 23, 2009; Mark Hibbs and Shahid-ur-Rehman, "Pakistan Civilian Fuel Cycle Plan Linked To NSG Trade Exception," *Nuclear Fuels*, August 27, 2007. Albright and Brannan argue that Pakistan may be constructing a fourth reactor at the Khushab site (David Albright and Paul Brannan, "Pakistan Doubling Rate of Making Nuclear Weapons: Time for Pakistan to Reverse Course," May 16, 2011).

[30] "Reprocessing" refers to the process of separating plutonium from spent nuclear fuel.

[31] Hibbs, June 15, 2000. According to a 1983 State Department document, the New Laboratories facility was "capable of extracting small quantities of plutonium," but large enough to "allow for expansion of reprocessing capacity." Available at http://www.gwu.edu/~nsarchiv/NSAEBB/NSAEBB114/chipak-11.pdf.

[32] David Albright and Paul Brannan, "Pakistan Expanding Plutonium Separation Facility Near Rawalpindi," Institute for Science and International Security, May 19, 2009. The 2001 Defense Department report stated that reprocessing (continued...)

at Chasma.[33] Pakistani plutonium-based nuclear warheads likely contain approximately 4-6 kilograms of plutonium, according to one expert estimate.[34]

Islamabad's construction of additional nuclear reactors and expansion of its reprocessing capabilities could indicate plans to increase and improve Pakistan's nuclear weapons arsenal in the near future. Indeed, then DIA Director Michael Maples told the Senate Armed Services Committee on March 10, 2009, that "Pakistan continues to develop its nuclear infrastructure, expand nuclear weapon stockpiles and seek more advanced warheads and delivery systems."[35] Similarly, Admiral Mullen confirmed during the May 14, 2009, hearing that the United States has "evidence" that Pakistan is expanding its nuclear arsenal. DIA Director Burgess's assessment during a March 10, 2011, hearing before the Senate Armed Services Committee was the same as his predecessor's.[36]

Responding to India?

The United Kingdom's Foreign and Commonwealth Office has argued that "Pakistan's strategic posture, including nuclear, is clearly framed around its perception of the threat from India."[37] Similarly, DIA Director Burgess told the Senate Armed Services Committee March 10, 2011, that the "persistent India-Pakistan rivalry drives Islamabad to develop its nuclear infrastructure, expand nuclear weapon stockpiles which are based primarily on highly enriched uranium, and seek more advanced nuclear warheads and delivery systems, including cruise missiles."[38]

Pakistan's Foreign Ministry stated February 2, 2011, that "Pakistan is mindful of the need to avoid arms race with India."[39] Nevertheless, Pakistan appears to be increasing its fissile production capability and improving its delivery vehicles in order to hedge against possible increases in India's nuclear arsenal. Islamabad may also accelerate its current nuclear weapons efforts. Air Commodore Khalid Banuri, Director of Arms Control and Disarmament Affairs in the SPD, asserted in December 2011 that Pakistan's "deterrence requirement remains dynamic" and a precise number of nuclear weapons to satisfy this requirement "cannot be quantified."[40] The government's National Command Authority (NCA) "expressed satisfaction" regarding "the pace of development and effectiveness of Pakistan's strategic deterrence," according to a December

---

(...continued)

facilities "are under construction," but did not identify any sites (*Proliferation: Threat and Response*, p. 27).

[33] David Albright and Paul Brannan, "Chashma Nuclear Site in Pakistan with Possible Reprocessing Plant," Institute for Science and International Security, January 18, 2007. Construction on the facility was begun during the 1970s with French assistance, but France cancelled its assistance for the project later that decade.

[34] Norris and Kristensen, 2011.

[35] Norris and Kristensen explain that plutonium reactors "provide the Pakistani military with several options: fabricating weapons that use plutonium cores, mixing plutonium with HEU to make composite cores, or using tritium to 'boost' the warheads' yield." (Norris and Kristensen, 2007).

[36] Burgess, World Wide Threat Assessment, March 10, 2011.

[37] Memorandum submitted by the Foreign and Commonwealth Office, October 1, 2008. Cited in House of Commons Foreign Affairs Committee, *Global Security: Non–Proliferation Fourth Report of Session 2008–09*, June 14, 2009.

[38] Burgess, World Wide Threat Assessment, March 10, 2011.

[39] Available at http://www.nti.org/e_research/source_docs/pakistan/ministry_foreign_affairs/1.pdf.

[40] Memorandum from Air Commodore Khalid Banuri, Director of Arms Control and Disarmament Affairs in the SPD, received by CRS analyst December 4, 2011.

14, 2010, statement.[41] Despite its increasing nuclear arsenal, Pakistan's Foreign Secretary stated in October 2007 that Pakistan "will not be the first to test [a nuclear explosive device] in our region."[42]

India has stated that it needs only a "credible minimum deterrent," but New Delhi has never defined what it means by such a deterrent and has refused to sign the Comprehensive Test Ban Treaty. Furthermore, both the 2008 U.S.-India nuclear cooperation agreement and associated 2008 decision by the Nuclear Suppliers Group (NSG) to exempt India from some of its export guidelines renewed New Delhi's access to the international uranium market. This access will result in more indigenous Indian uranium available for weapons because it will not be consumed by India's newly safeguarded reactors.[43] Pakistani officials have offered estimates for the number of additional nuclear weapons that New Delhi could build. For example, Wajid Shamsul Hasan, Pakistan's High Commissioner to the United Kingdom, argued in an October 2010 letter to a British newspaper that eight Indian nuclear reactors that will not be subject to International Atomic Energy Agency (IAEA) safeguards have the potential to produce 280 nuclear weapons annually.[44] India currently has approximately 60-80 nuclear weapons, according to one public estimate.[45] [46]

Pakistani officials have stated that the government may need to increase significantly its nuclear arsenal in response to possible Indian plans to do the same. According to an April 2006 television broadcast, Pakistani officials from the government's NCA expressed "concern" that the 2008 U.S.-India nuclear cooperation agreement could tilt the strategic balance between India and Pakistan in favor of the former. The officials suggested that Islamabad may need to increase or improve its nuclear arsenal in order to "to meet all requirements of minimum credible defence deterrence."[47] (See the "Nuclear Doctrine" section for more on Pakistan's deterrence concept.) Similarly, Pakistan's Permanent Representative to the IAEA wrote in July 2008 that the agreement could cause a nuclear arms race between Pakistan and India.[48] Moreover, a Foreign Ministry spokesperson indicated during a May 21, 2009, press briefing that, despite the

---

[41] "Meeting of the National Command Authority," *Pakistan Official News*, December 14, 2010.

[42] Statement by Foreign Secretary, Riaz Mohammad Khan, at the General Debate of the 62nd Session of the UN General Assembly, October 2, 2007. Gary Samore included Pakistan in a list of countries "where testing might make sense in terms of" their nuclear weapons programs (*Arms Control Today*, May 2011). In August 2003 responses to questions for the record from the Senate Select Committee on Intelligence, the CIA stated that Pakistan "almost certainly would conduct nuclear testing in reaction to an Indian nuclear test." However, Dr. Rifaat Hussain of Quad-i-Azam University in Islamabad stated that it is "extremely unlikely" that, absent additional Indian nuclear tests, Pakistan will test nuclear weapons (personal e-mail, October 6, 2011).

[43] See CRS Report RL33016, *U.S. Nuclear Cooperation with India: Issues for Congress*, by Paul K. Kerr.

[44] "Pakistan for Reducing Existing Stocks of Fissile Material: Wajid," *Associated Press of Pakistan*, October 19, 2010. If Hasan's estimate assumes that Indian weapons designers could build weapons which would each contain approximately 4.5 kilograms of reactor-grade plutonium, then the estimate would be roughly consistent with a 2006 estimate that these reactors could produce 1,250 kilograms of reactor-grade plutonium per year (see Mian et al., 2006).

[45] Robert Norris and Hans Kristensen, "Nuclear Notebook: Indian Nuclear Forces, 2010," *Bulletin of the Atomic Scientists*, September/October 2010.

[46] James N. Miller, Principal Deputy Under Secretary of Defense for Policy, told the House Committee on Armed Services in November 2011 that "China is increasing the size of its nuclear arsenal but is estimated to have only a few hundred nuclear weapons. India and Pakistan are also increasing the size of their nuclear arsenals, but each is estimated to have fewer weapons than China." (*Statement of Dr. James N. Miller, Principal Deputy Under Secretary of Defense for Policy, Before The House Committee On Armed Services*, November 2, 2011.)

[47] "Pakistan Command Meeting Voices Concern Over Indo-US Nuclear Deal," *Pakistan TV*, April 12, 2006.

[48] Available at http://verificationthoughts.blogspot.com/2008/07/indian-separation-plan.html.

---

government's continued opposition to a "nuclear or conventional arms race in South Asia," Pakistan may need to increase its nuclear arsenal in response to Indian conventional and nuclear arms expansion. Dr. Syed Rifaat Hussain of Quad-i-Azam University in Islamabad argued in 2011 that "Pakistan would need three to four years to gain enough plutonium stocks to maintain a credible posture of nuclear deterrence" versus India.[49]

Illustrating this point, a Pakistani Foreign Office spokesperson reacted to India's July 26, 2009, launch of its first indigenously built nuclear-powered submarine by asserting that "continued induction of new lethal weapon systems by India is detrimental to regional peace and stability," adding that "[w]ithout entering into an arms race with India, Pakistan will take all appropriate steps to safeguard its security and maintain strategic balance in South Asia." The Indian submarine, which is not yet deployed, will reportedly be capable of carrying nuclear-armed ballistic missiles.[50] Admiral Mohammad Asif Sandila, the Chief of Pakistan's Naval Staff, announced "the formal establishment of the Naval Strategic Force Command of Pakistan" on May 19, 2012.[51] Describing the Strategic Force as "the custodian of the nation's 2nd strike capability," Sandila argued that it "will strengthen Pakistan's policy of Credible Minimum Deterrence and ensure regional stability," but he did not elaborate.

Similarly, according to the January 2010 statement, the NCA identified "developments detrimental to the objectives of strategic stability in the region," including India's acquisition of "advanced weapons systems" and missile defense systems. The NCA also noted that the 2008 NSG decision described above, as well as subsequent nuclear fuel supply agreements that New Delhi has concluded with several governments, "would enable India to produce substantial quantities of fissile material for nuclear weapons by freeing up its domestic resources." The statement suggests that Pakistan could increase or improve its nuclear weapons in response to these developments, but does not explicitly say so. Shahzad Chaudhry, a retired Pakistani Air Vice Marshall, argued during a July 18, 2011, U.S. Institute of Peace event that India's stockpile of reactor-grade plutonium is an additional concern for Pakistan.[52]

Whether and to what extent Pakistan's current expansion of its nuclear weapons-related facilities is a response to the U.S.-India agreement is unclear, partly because descriptions of the government's decisions regarding those facilities are not publicly available. However, Air Commodore Banuri argued in December 2011 that "India's massive conventional military build up, the India-U.S. nuclear deal," and India's pursuit of missile defense systems, forced Pakistan "to make qualitative and quantitative adjustments."[53] Banuri also cited Indian military doctrines that Islamabad describes as prescribing rapid conventional military action against Pakistan.

---

[49] Personal e-mail, October 6, 2011.

[50] Bappa Majumdar, "India Launches Its First Nuclear-Powered Submarine," *Reuters*, July 26, 2009; Nasir Jaffry, "Pakistan Hits Out At 'Detrimental' Indian Nuclear Sub," *Agence France Presse*, July 28, 2009; "Induction Of Indigenous Nuke Sub Into Navy Longway Off: Experts," *The Press Trust of India*, July 26, 2009; "N-Submarine Still Wrapped In Secrecy," *Indo-Asian News Service*, July 27, 2009.

[51] "Naval Chief Inaugurates Naval Strategic Force Headquarters," *Inter Services Public Relations*, May 19, 2012.

[52] For details about India's reactor-grade plutonium, see "International Panel on Fissile Materials, Global Fissile Material Report 2010: Balancing the Books: Production and Stocks," p. 120-122, http://www.fissilematerials.org/ipfm/site_down/gfmr10.pdf. Reactor-grade plutonium can be used as fissile material in nuclear weapons; see U.S. Committee on the Internationalization of the Civilian Nuclear Fuel Cycle; Committee on International Security and Arms Control, Policy and Global Affairs Division; National Academy of Sciences and National Research Council, *Internationalization of the Nuclear Fuel Cycle: Goals, Strategies, and Challenges*, 2008, p. 17.

[53] Memorandum from Air Commodore Khalid Banuri, Director of Arms Control and Disarmament Affairs in the SPD, (continued...)

In addition to making qualitative and quantitative improvements to its nuclear arsenal, Pakistan could increase the number of circumstances under which it would be willing to use nuclear weapons. For example, Peter Lavoy has argued that India's efforts to improve its conventional military capabilities could enable New Delhi to achieve "technical superiority" in intelligence, surveillance, and reconnaissance, as well as precision targeting, providing India with "the capability to effectively locate and efficiently destroy strategically important targets in Pakistan."[54] Islamabad could respond by lowering the threshold for using nuclear weapons, according to Lavoy. Indeed, a Pakistan Foreign Ministry spokesperson warned in May 2009 that Islamabad could take this step. (See the "Nuclear Doctrine" section.) The Pakistani government may also consider fielding non-strategic nuclear weapons in order to increase the credibility of its nuclear deterrent versus Indian conventional military operations.[55] On April 19, 2011, Lieutenant General (Retired) Khalid Ahmed Kidwai, Director General of Pakistan's Strategic Plans Division, described the first test of a new nuclear-capable ballistic missile as "a very important milestone in consolidating Pakistan's strategic deterrence capability at all levels of the threat spectrum" (see "Delivery Vehicles" section below).[56]

Fissile Material Cutoff Treaty

Pakistani officials cite their concern about India's recently acquired ability to expand its nuclear arsenal as a reason for refusing to support negotiations in the Conference on Disarmament (CD), which operates by consensus, on a Fissile Material Cutoff Treaty (FMCT).[57] The CD adopted a program of work[58] in May 2009 that established a working group charged with negotiating an FMCT on the basis of the 1995 "Shannon Mandate."[59] Although Pakistan supported the work plan in 2009, it did not support the adoption of a draft program of work for 2010.[60] Ambassador Zamir Akram, Pakistan's Permanent Representative to the CD, stated February 18, 2010, that Islamabad had supported the 2009 program of work[61] because the government had believed that the Obama Administration might reverse U.S. policy on nuclear cooperation with India.

(...continued)

received by CRS analyst December 4, 2011.

[54] Peter Lavoy, "Islamabad's Nuclear Posture: Its Premises and Implementation," in *Pakistan's Nuclear Future: Worries Beyond War*, Henry Sokolski, Ed. (Carlisle, PA: Strategic Studies Institute) January 2008. p. 158.

[55] Rezaul H Laskar, "Pak's New Nuke Missile Aimed at India's 'Cold Start' Doctrine," *The Press Trust of India Limited*, April 20, 2011; "Nasr Missile Shatters India's Dream of Limited War," *Nawa-e Waqt (BBC Monitoring South Asia)*, April 20, 2011; Sanjeev Miglani, "Pakistan Builds Low Yield Nuclear Capability, Concern Grows," *Reuters*, May 15, 2011.

[56] Inter Services Public Relations Press release No PR94/2011-ISPR, April 19, 2011.

[57] For more information about the treaty, see CRS Report RL33865, *Arms Control and Nonproliferation: A Catalog of Treaties and Agreements*, by Amy F. Woolf, Mary Beth Nikitin, and Paul K. Kerr.

[58] Decision for the Establishment of a Programme of Work for the 2009 Session, Conference on Disarmament, CD/1864, May 29, 2009.

[59] Report of Ambassador Gerald E. Shannon of Canada on Consultations on the Most Appropriate Arrangement to Negotiate a Treaty Banning the Production of Fissile Material for Nuclear Weapons or Other Nuclear Explosive Devices, CD/1299, March 24, 1995. Available at http://www.reachingcriticalwill.org/political/cd/shannon.html.

[60] Draft Decision for the Establishment of a Programme of Work for the 2010 Session, Conference on Disarmament, CD/1889, July 6, 2010. Also see Statement by Ambassador Zamir Akram, Permanent Representative of Pakistan to the Conference on Disarmament, August 31, 2010.

[61] Statement by Ambassador Zamir Akram, February 18, 2010.

Pakistan, which is widely regarded as the main opponent to the start of negotiations,[62] argues that a treaty on fissile material should not only prohibit the production of new material, but should also require states with such material to reduce their stocks.[63] A treaty without such a requirement, according to Pakistan, will put the country at a disadvantage with respect to India because of what Islamabad characterizes as New Delhi's larger fissile material stocks and production capability.[64] Although the Shannon Mandate states that it "does not preclude any delegation" from proposing the inclusion of existing stocks in the negotiations, Islamabad argues that the CD ought to determine the treaty's scope prior to beginning negotiations.[65] Akram stated June 1, 2011, that Pakistan had not changed its position on this question. But he said in an October 2011 interview that Islamabad would be wiling to negotiate an FMCT under the Shannon Mandate if the NSG were to give Pakistan a waiver similar to the one received by India.[66]

Delivery Vehicles

Pakistan has two types of delivery vehicles for nuclear weapons: aircraft controlled by the Pakistan Air Force and surface-to-surface missiles controlled by the Pakistan Army. Pakistan could deliver its nuclear weapons using F-16 fighter aircraft purchased from the United States, provided that modifications are made. It is widely believed that Islamabad has made the relevant modifications to the F-16s previously sold to them by Washington.[67] Although concerns have been raised about the impact of these sales on the strategic balance in South Asia,[68] the U.S. government maintains that the sale of additional F-16s to Pakistan will not alter the regional balance of power.[69] The contract for provision of an additional 18 aircraft was signed in 2006, as was the contract for the weapons for those aircraft and a contract to perform the mid-life upgrade on Pakistan's F-16A/B model aircraft.[70] Pakistan's F-16 fleet will, therefore, be expanded, but it is unclear what portion of the fleet will be capable of a nuclear mission. Mirage V aircraft may also be used as delivery vehicles.[71]

---

[62] Zia Mian and A.H. Nayyar, "Playing the Nuclear Game: Pakistan and the Fissile Material Cutoff Treaty," *Arms Control Today*, April 2010.

[63] Akram, February 18, 2010.

[64] Ibid. See also Mr. Raza Basltmir Tarpar, Acting Permanent Representative of Pakistan to the United Nations, Statement at the General Assembly, July 27, 2011, available at http://www reachingcriticalwill.org/political/cd/2011/statements/plenary/280711_Pakistan.pdf.

[65] Akram, August 31, 2010.

[66] Tom Z. Collina and Daniel Horner, "The South Asian Nuclear Balance: An Interview with Pakistani Ambassador to the CD Zamir Akram," *Arms Control Today*, December 2011.

[67] The 1993 National Security Council report indicated that Pakistan would use these aircraft to deliver nuclear weapons. See National Security Council, *Report to Congress*.

[68] CRS Report RL33515, *Combat Aircraft Sales to South Asia: Potential Implications*, by Christopher Bolkcom, Richard F. Grimmett, and K. Alan Kronstadt; Zachary Ginsburg, "US Renews Fighter Exports to Pakistan," *Arms Control Today*, September 2007. http://www.armscontrol.org/act/2007_09/USPakistan.asp.

[69] "Release of these systems would not significantly reduce India's quantitative or qualitative military advantage. Release of these modifications to Pakistan will neither affect the regional balance of power nor introduce a new technology as this level of capability or higher already exists in other countries in the region." Defense Security and Cooperation Agency news release, June 28, 2006. http://www.dsca.mil/PressReleases/36-b/2006/Pakistan_06-11.pdf.

[70] Pakistan has not exercised its option to purchase an additional 18 F-16 fighter aircraft (see CRS Report RS22757, *U.S. Arms Sales to Pakistan*).

[71] Norris and Kristensen, 2009; Salik, Naeem, *The Genesis of South Asian Nuclear Deterrence: Pakistan's Perspective*, (Oxford: Oxford University Press), 2009, p. 215.

DIA Director Burgess told the Senate Armed Services Committee March 10, 2011, that Pakistan is developing new missile systems which, when deployed and added to Islamabad's current ballistic missiles, will enable Pakistan "to strike a variety of targets at ranges of 200-2000 kilometers with both conventional and nuclear payloads."[72] Islamabad has three types of ballistic missiles[73] thought to be nuclear-capable: the solid-fuel *Hatf-III* (*Ghaznavi*), with a range of approximately 300-400 kilometers[74]; the solid-fuel *Hatf-IV* (*Shaheen*), with a range of over 450 kilometers[75]; and the liquid-fuel *Hatf-V* (*Ghauri*), with an approximate range of almost 1,300 kilometers.[76] Pakistan tested "an improved version" of the Shaheen missile, called the Shaheen-1A, April 25, 2012, according to an announcement from Pakistan's Inter Services Public Relations, which described the missile as having "improvements in range and technical parameters."[77] The announcement did not specify a range, but described the Shaheen-1A as an "Intermediate Range Ballistic Missile," suggesting that the missile's range could be at least 3,000 kilometers.[78] The solid-fuel nuclear-capable *Hatf-VI* (*Shaheen-2*) missile, when deployed, will be "capable of reaching targets out to 2,000 kilometers," former DIA Director Maples stated March 10, 2009,[79] adding that Islamabad has made "significant progress" on the missile. A 2009 National Air and Space Intelligence Center (NASIC) report appears to support this conclusion, stating that the missile "probably will soon be deployed." Pakistan's Inter Services Public Relations announced April 19, 2011, the first successful flight test of a "newly developed Short Range Surface to Surface Multi Tube Ballistic Missile Hatf IX (NASR)." The missile has a range of 60 kilometers and "carries nuclear warheads of appropriate yield with high accuracy," according to the press release.[80] Islamabad continues to carry out ballistic missile tests, but

---

[72] Burgess, World Wide Threat Assessment, March 10, 2011.

[73] All ballistic missiles described in this paragraph are road-mobile. Unless otherwise noted, ranges are from National Air and Space Intelligence Center, *Ballistic and Cruise Missile Threat*, 2009.

[74] A May 2010 Pakistani press release gave the range as 290 kilometers. (Press Release No 186/2010: "Prime Minister Syed Yousaf Raza Gillani Addressing the Occasion After Successful Training Launches of a Short Range Ballistic Missile Hatf III (GHAZNAVI) and a Medium Range Ballistic Missile Hatf IV (SHAHEEN 1) on Saturday," *Inter Services Public Relations*, May 8, 2010).

[75] Dr. Samar Mubarakmand, Chairman of Pakistan's National Engineering and Scientific Commission, gave the missile's range as 700 kilometers during a 2004 television interview ("Capital Talk Special," *GEO-TV*, May 3, 2004). A January 2008 Pakistani press release also gave the range as 700 kilometers (*Inter-Services Public Relations*, January 25, 2008). However, a May 2010 Pakistani press release gave the range as 650 kilometers (*Inter Services Public Relations*, May 8, 2010).

[76] A February 2008 Pakistani press release also gives the range as 1,300 kilometers. (*Inter-Services Public Relations*, No 35/2008-ISPR, February 1, 2008).

[77] Inter Services Public Relations Press release No PR98/2012-ISPR, April 25, 2012. Available at http://www.ispr.gov.pk/front/main.asp?o=t-press_release&date=2012/4/25.

[78] According to the National Air and Space Intelligence Center, an Intermediate-Range Ballistic Missile has a range of 3,000-5,500 kilometers.

[79] See also, Nuclear Notebook, 2009, "Worldwide Ballistic Missile Inventories," *Arms Control Today Fact Sheet*, http://www.armscontrol.org/factsheets/missiles.asp; and Mahmud Ali Durrani, "Pakistan's Strategic Thinking and the Role of Nuclear Weapons," *Cooperative Monitoring Center Occasional Paper 37*, July 2004. http://www.cmc.sandia.gov/cmc-papers/sand2004-3375p.pdf. Mubarakmand gave the missile's range as 2,500 kilometers in the 2004 interview. An April 2008 Pakistani press release gave the range as 2,000 kilometers (Inter-Services Public Relations "Review of 61st Formation Commanders Conference being presided by the Chief of Army Staff, General Ashfaq Parvez Kayani at General Headquarters on Monday," No 27/2008-ISPR, April 21, 2008).

[80] Inter Services Public Relations Press release No PR94/2011-ISPR, April 19, 2011. Available at http://www.ispr.gov.pk/front/main.asp?o=t-press_release&id=1721.

---

notifies India in advance in accordance with an October 2005 bilateral missile pre-notification pact.[81]

Maples also indicated that Pakistan is developing nuclear-capable cruise missiles: the Babur (ground-launched) and the Ra'ad (air-launched), both of which will have estimated ranges of 320 kilometers, according to the NASIC report.[82] In an April 29, 2011, announcement of a successful flight test of the Ra'ad, the Pakistani government gave the missile's range as 350 kilometers.[83] In an October 28, 2011, announcement of a flight test of the Babur, the Pakistani government gave the missile's range as 700 kilometers.[84]

Nuclear Doctrine

Pakistan's strategic doctrine is undeclared, and will probably remain so, but prominent officials and analysts have offered insights concerning its basic tenets.[85] Describing the guiding principle as minimum credible nuclear deterrence,[86] high-level officials' statements point to four policy objectives for Islamabad's nuclear weapons: deter all forms of external aggression; deter through a combination of conventional and strategic forces; deter counterforce strategies by securing strategic assets and threatening nuclear retaliation; and stabilize strategic deterrence in South Asia.[87] Pakistani officials have also indicated that this nuclear posture is designed to preserve territorial integrity against Indian attack, prevent military escalation, and counter its main rival's conventional superiority.[88] Banuri explained in December 2011 Islamabad's nuclear arsenal is part of an effort "to deny India the space for launching any kind of aggression against Pakistan."[89]

Pakistan has pledged no-first-use against non-nuclear-weapon states, but has not ruled out first-use against a nuclear-armed aggressor, such as India.[90] Some analysts say this ambiguity serves to

---

[81] "Agreement Between the Republic of India and the Islamic Republic of Pakistan on Pre-Notification of Flight Testing of Ballistic Missiles." Full text on the Henry L. Stimson Center website: http://www.stimson.org/?SN= SA20060207949.

[82] National Air and Space Intelligence Center, 2009.

[83] "Pakistan: New Cruise Missile Capable of Carrying Nuclear Warheads," *Associated Press of Pakistan*, April 29, 2011.

[84] Inter Services Public Relations Press Note, "Pakistan Successfully Test Fires Multi-Tube Stealth Cruise Missile," October 28, 2011.

[85] Peter Lavoy, "Pakistan's Nuclear Posture: Security and Survivability," Paper presented to the Conference on Pakistan's Nuclear Future, Nonproliferation Education Center, Washington, DC, April 28, 2006: http://www npec-web.org/Frameset.asp?PageType=Single&PDFFile=20070121-Lavoy-PakistanNuclearPosture&PDFFolder=Essays.

[86] A January 13, 2010, statement describing a National Command Authority meeting refers to Pakistan's "policy of credible minimum deterrence."

[87] Durrani, 2004.

[88] For an in-depth discussion of minimum deterrence, see Naeem Salik, "Minimum Deterrence and India Pakistan Nuclear Dialogue: Case Study on Pakistan," Landau Network Centro Volta South Asia Security Project Case Study, January 2006. http://www.centrovolta.it/landau/ South%20Asia%20Security%20Program_file%5CDocumenti%5CCase%20Studies%5CSalik%20- %20S.A.%20Case%20Study%202006.pdf.

[89] Memorandum from Air Commodore Khalid Banuri, Director of Arms Control and Disarmament Affairs in the SPD, received by CRS analyst December 4, 2011.

[90] Ibid. It is worth noting that President Zardari stated in late 2008 that Pakistan would not be the first to use nuclear weapons against India. See James Lamont and Farhan Bokhari, "Pakistan In Trade And Arms Offer To India," *Financial Times*, November 23, 2008; "Pakistan Against Use Of Nuclear Weapons: Zardari," *Associated Press of* (continued...)

---

maintain deterrence against India's conventional superiority; the Foreign Ministry spokesperson stated May 21, 2009, that "there are acquisitions of sophisticated weaponry by our neighbour which will disturb the conventional balance between our two countries and hence, lower the nuclear threshold." Other analysts argue that keeping the first-use option against New Delhi allows Islamabad to conduct sub-conventional operations, such as support for low intensity conflict or proxy war in Kashmir, while effectively deterring India at the strategic level.[91] Pakistan has reportedly addressed issues of survivability through pursuing a second strike capability, possibly building hard and deeply buried storage and launch facilities, deploying road-mobile missiles, deploying air defenses around strategic sites, and utilizing concealment measures.[92]

Pakistani statements suggest that the government has a high threshold for using nuclear weapons. According to a March 2012 State Department report, "Pakistan previously has said it would not be the first to resume nuclear testing and that nuclear use would be a 'last resort' under circumstances that are 'unthinkable.'"[93]

Command and Control

Pakistan's command and control over its nuclear weapons is compartmentalized and includes strict operational security. The government's command and control system is based on "C4I2SR" (command, control, communication, computers, intelligence, information, surveillance and reconnaissance). Islamabad's Strategic Command Organization has a three-tiered structure, consisting of the National Command Authority (NCA), the Strategic Plans Division (SPD), and the Strategic Forces Commands.

The NCA, established in 2000, supervises the functions and administration of all of Pakistan's organizations involved in nuclear weapons research, development, and employment, as well as the military services that operate the strategic forces.[94] The prime minister, as head of government, is chairperson of the NCA.[95] The NCA also includes the chair of the joint chiefs of staff; the ministers of defense, interior, and finance; the director general of the SPD; and the

---

(...continued)

Pakistan, November 22, 2008; "Interview with President Asif Ali Zardari," CNN Larry King Live, December 2, 2008.

[91] Kanti Bajpai, "No First Use in the India-Pakistan Context," *Pugwash Workshop No. 279*, November 2002. http://www.pugwash.org/reports/nw/bajpai htm.

[92] Lavoy, 2006.

[93] *Report To Congress: Update on Progress toward Regional Nuclear Nonproliferation in South Asia*, submitted March 20, 2012.

[94] December 2007 Ordinance to Provide for the Constitution and Establishment of National Command Authority.

[95] When the NCA was established in 2000, the government's announcement designated the Head of Government, or Prime Minister, as Chairperson. At that time, General Musharraf, as Chief Executive, became Chairperson and stayed in that position after becoming President in 2002. He appointed the Prime Minister as Vice Chairman. However, President Zardari returned the NCA to its original structure when, in a November 2009 re-promulgation of the 2007 NCA Ordinance, he specified that the Prime Minister would be Chairperson, removing himself from that position (this re-promulgation also abolished the position of Vice Chairman). Zardari may have done this in reaction to Parliamentary pressure, and perhaps to boost his waning political support. According to Brigadier General (Ret.) Naeem Salik, the change in Chairmanship may have only a symbolic impact on nuclear policy-making, since no changes were made to the Strategic Plans Division itself. The Pakistani Parliament is now considering a bill, the National Command Bill of 2009, which includes these provisions, and could add reporting requirements on the safety and security of Pakistan's nuclear assets. A July 2009 Supreme Court decision required that the Ordinances from the Musharraf era be made law.

commanders of the Army, Air Force, and Navy. The final authority to launch a nuclear strike requires consensus within the NCA; the chairperson must cast the final vote. The NCA is comprised of two committees, the Employment Control Committee (ECC) and the Development Control Committee (DCC), each of which includes a mix of civilian and military officials. The ECC's functions include establishing a command and control system over the use of nuclear weapons. The DCC "exercises technical, financial and administrative control over all strategic organisations, including national laboratories and research and development organisations associated with the development and modernisation of nuclear weapons."[96]

The SPD is headed by a director general from the Army and acts as the secretariat for the NCA. The SPD's functions include formulating Islamabad's nuclear policy, strategy, and doctrine; developing the nuclear chain of command; and formulating operational plans at the service level for the movement, deployment, and use of nuclear weapons. The Army, Air Force, and Navy each have their own strategic force command, but operational planning and control remains with the NCA. The SPD coordinates operational plans with the strategic forces commands. According to current and former Pakistani officials, Islamabad employs a system which requires that at least two, and perhaps three, people authenticate launch codes for nuclear weapons.[97]

On December 13, 2007, then-President Musharraf formalized these authorities and structure in the "National Command Authority Ordinance, 2007."[98] The NCA was established by administrative order, but now has a legal basis. Analysts point out that the timing of this ordinance was meant to help the command and control system weather political transitions and potentially preserve the military's strong control over the system. The ordinance also addresses the problems of the proliferation of nuclear expertise and personnel reliability. It outlines punishable offenses related to breach of confidentiality or leakage of "secured information," gives the SPD authority to investigate suspicious conduct, states that punishment for these offenses can be up to 25 years imprisonment, and applies to both serving and retired personnel, including military personnel, notwithstanding any other laws. As a result, Pakistani authorities say that the ordinance should strengthen their control over strategic organizations and their personnel.

Security Concerns

According to a 2001 Department of Defense report, Islamabad's nuclear weapons "are probably stored in component form,"[99] which suggests that the nuclear warheads are stored separately from delivery vehicles. According to some reports, the fissile cores of the weapons are separated from

---

[96] *Nuclear Black Markets: Pakistan, A.Q. Khan and the Rise of Proliferation Networks,* (London: The International Institute for Strategic Studies), 2007, p. 111; Pakistan Announcement of Nuclear-Weapons Command-and-Control Mechanism, Associated Press of Pakistan, February 3, 2000. *Nuclear Black Markets,* pp. 110-111, has organization charts of the NCA and SPD.

[97] See P. Cotta-Ramusino and M. Martellini, "Nuclear Safety, Nuclear Stability And Nuclear Strategy In Pakistan: A Concise Report Of A Visit By Landau Network - Centro Volta," January 14, 2002. Available at http://www.pugwash.org/september11/pakistan-nuclear.htm; Kenneth N. Luongo and Brig. Gen. (Ret.) Naeem Salik, "Building Confidence in Pakistan's Nuclear Security," *Arms Control Today,* December 2007; Robin Walker, "Pakistan's Evolution as a Nuclear Weapons State: Lt. Gen. Khalid Kidwai's CCC Address, *Strategic Insights,* November 1, 2006.

[98] "President Promulgated National Command Authority Ordinance," *Associated Press of Pakistan,* December 13, 2007.

[99] *Proliferation: Threat and Response,* p. 27.

---

the non-nuclear explosives.[100] But whether this is actually the case is unclear; one report states that the warheads and delivery vehicles are probably stored separately in facilities close to one another, but says nothing about the fissile cores.[101] And, according to an account of a 2008 experts' group visit to Pakistan, Lieutenant General Khalid Kidwai, the head of the SPD, suggested that the nuclear warheads (containing the fissile cores) may be mated with their delivery vehicles.[102] According to Kidwai, the report says, the SPD's official position is that the weapons "will be ready when required, at the shortest notice; [but] the Pakistani doctrine is not endorsing a US-USSR model with weapons on hair trigger alert." The 2001 Defense Department report says that Pakistan can probably assemble its weapons fairly quickly.[103]

It warrants mention that, although separate storage may provide a layer of protection against accidental launch or prevent theft of an assembled weapon, it may be easier for unauthorized people to remove a weapon's fissile material core if it is not assembled. Dispersal of the assets may also create more potential access points for acquisition and may increase the risk of diversion.[104]

As the United States prepared to launch an attack on the Afghan Taliban after September 11, 2001, President Musharraf reportedly ordered that Pakistan's nuclear arsenal be redeployed to "at least six secret new locations."[105] This action came at a time of uncertainly about the future of the region, including the direction of U.S.-Pakistan relations. Islamabad's leadership was uncertain whether the United States would decide to conduct military strikes against Pakistan's nuclear assets if the government did not assist the United States against the Taliban. Indeed, President Musharraf cited protection of Pakistan's nuclear and missile assets as one of the reasons for Islamabad's dramatic policy shift.[106]

These events, in combination with the 1999 Kargil crisis, the 2002 conflict with India at the Line of Control, and revelations about the A. Q. Khan proliferation network, inspired a variety of reforms to secure the nuclear complex. Risk of nuclear war in South Asia ran high in the 1999 Kargil crisis, when the Pakistani military is believed to have begun preparing nuclear-tipped

---

[100] Joby Warrick, "Pakistan Nuclear Security Questioned; Lack of Knowledge About Arsenal May Limit U.S. Options," *Washington Post*, November 11, 2007; Peter Wonacott, "Inside Pakistan's Drive To Guard Its A-Bombs," *Wall Street Journal*, November 29, 2007; David E. Sanger, "Trust Us: So, What About Those Nukes?," *New York Times*, November 11, 2007; *Nuclear Black Markets*, 2007, p.33; Cotta-Ramusino and Martellini, 2002. See also, George Perkovich of the Carnegie Endowment for International Peace quoted in Nigel Hawkes, "Pakistan Could Lose Control of its Arsenal," *The Times (London)*, September 20, 2001.

[101] Lavoy, "Islamabad's Nuclear Posture: Its Premises and Implementation." p. 141.

[102] Maurizio Martellini, "Security and Safety Issues about the Nuclear Complex: Pakistan's Standpoints. A Concise Report of a Visit to Islamabad by Landau Network Centro Volta (LNCV) Mission Carried out on February 9-13 2008."

[103] *Proliferation: Threat and Response*, p. 28.

[104] See Graham Allison, "What About the Nukes?" *Newsweek Web*, December 28, 2007. http://www.newsweek.com/id/82259

[105] Molly Moore and Kamran Khan, "Pakistan Moves Nuclear Weapons - Musharraf Says Arsenal Is Now Secure," *Washington Post*, November 11, 2001.

[106] "Partial transcript of Pakistan President Musharraf's televised speech asking the people of Pakistan to support his course of action," September 19, 2001. http://www.washingtonpost.com/wp-srv/nation/specials/attacked/transcripts/pakistantext_091901 html.

---

missiles.[107] It should be noted that, even at the high alert levels of 2001 and 2002, there were no reports of Pakistan mating the warheads with delivery systems.[108]

In the fall of 2007 and early 2008, some observers expressed concern about the security of the country's arsenal if political instability were to persist.[109] Former Prime Minister Benazir Bhutto said in a November 5, 2007, interview that, although then-President Musharraf claimed to be in firm control of the nuclear arsenal, she feared this control could weaken due to instability in the country.[110] Similarly, Michael Krepon of the Henry L. Stimson Center has argued that "a prolonged period of turbulence and infighting among the country's President, Prime Minister, and Army Chief" could jeopardize the army's unity of command, which "is essential for nuclear security."[111] During that time, U.S. military officials also expressed concern about the security of Pakistan's nuclear weapons.[112] Then-IAEA Director General Mohamed ElBaradei also has expressed fears that a radical regime could take power in Pakistan, and thereby acquire nuclear weapons.[113] Experts also worry that while nuclear weapons are currently under firm control, with warheads disassembled, technology could be sold off by insiders during a worsened crisis.[114]

However, U.S. intelligence officials have expressed greater confidence regarding the security of Islamabad's nuclear weapons. Deputy Secretary of State John D. Negroponte in testimony to Congress on November 7, 2007, said he believed that there is "plenty of succession planning that's going on in the Pakistani military" and that Pakistan's nuclear weapons are under "effective technical control."[115] Similarly, Donald Kerr, Principal Deputy Director of National Intelligence, told a Washington audience May 29, 2008, that the Pakistani military's control of the nuclear weapons is "a good thing because that's an institution in Pakistan that has, in fact, withstood many of the political changes over the years." More recently, former DIA Director Maples stated March 10, 2009, that Islamabad "has taken important steps to safeguard its nuclear weapons," although he pointed out that "vulnerabilities exist." As noted, current DIA Director Burgess articulated a similar assessment in March 2011.

As noted, other U.S. officials have also conveyed confidence in the security of Islamabad's nuclear weapons. General Petraeus stated on May 10, 2009, that "[w]ith respect to the—the nuclear weapons and—and sites that are controlled by Pakistan … we have confidence in their security procedures and elements and believe that the security of those sites is adequate."[116]

---

[107] Bruce Riedel, "American Diplomacy and the 1999 Kargil Summit at Blair House," Center for the Advanced Study of India, Policy Paper Series, 2002. http://www.ccc.nps navy.mil/research/kargil/reidel.pdf.

[108] Lavoy, 2006.

[109] "Opinions Mixed on Pakistani Nuclear Security," *Global Security Newswire*, November 6, 2007. http://www.nti.org/d_newswire/issues/recent_stories.asp?category=nuclear#6783E660.

[110] Also see comments by David Albright in the same interview ("Pakistan in Crisis: Interview with Benazir Bhutto," *CNN,* November 5, 2007).

[111] "U.S.-Pakistan Strategic Relations," Statement before the Committee on Senate Homeland Security and Governmental Affairs Subcommittee on Federal Financial Management, Government Information, Federal Services, and International Security June 12, 2008.

[112] "Lieutenant General Carter Ham Holds a Defense Department Briefing," *CQ Transcripts*, November 7, 2007.

[113] "Al Baradei to Al Hayat," *Dar Al Hayat*, English Edition online, January 10, 2008, http://english.daralhayat.com/Spec/01-2008/Article-20080110-639032eb-c0a8-10ed-01ae-81ab2ea588db/story html.

[114] Also see comments by David Albright in "Pakistan in Crisis," 2007.

[115] House Foreign Affairs Committee Hearing on Democracy, Authoritarianism and Terrorism in Contemporary Pakistan, November 7, 2007.

[116] Interview with General David H. Petraeus, *FOX News Sunday*, May 10, 2009. http://www foxnews.com/story/ (continued...)

Admiral Mullen echoed this assessment during a May 14, 2009, hearing before the Senate Armed Services Committee. More recently, Secretary of Defense Robert Gates stated in a January 21, 2010, interview that the United States is "very comfortable with the security of Pakistan's nuclear weapons."[117] Then-State Department spokesperson P.J. Crowley told reporters April 9, 2010, that Pakistan "has demonstrated that it can secure its own nuclear weapons program." Similarly, Under Secretary of Defense Michele Flournoy stated during an April 29, 2010, hearing that "we believe that Pakistan has a very solid command-and-control system for their nuclear weapons," adding that "they have made a great deal of investment in the security of their nuclear arsenal."[118] As noted, this confidence has continued into 2011 and 2012. James Clapper, Director of National Intelligence, told the House Intelligence Committee February 10, 2011, that "our assessment is that the nuclear weapons in Pakistan are secure." General Petraeus told the Senate Armed Services Committee March 15, 2011, that "[t]here is quite considerable security for the Pakistani nuclear weapons." Asked about the security of Pakistan's weapons following a May 2011 insurgent attack on a military installation in Karachi, Assistant Secretary of State Robert Blake stated June 21, 2011, that "there is much more heightened security around" Pakistan's nuclear weapons facilities than at the Karachi installation. More recently, Clapper expressed confidence during a February 16, 2012, Senate Armed Services Committee hearing that Pakistan is willing and able to protect its nuclear arsenal.

U.S. knowledge of Pakistan's arsenal, however, remains limited, according to U.S. officials. For example, Mullen stated that "we're limited in what we actually know" about Islamabad's nuclear arsenal. Leon Panetta, Director of the Central Intelligence Agency, similarly acknowledged in a May 18, 2010, speech that the United States does not possess the intelligence to locate all of Pakistan's nuclear weapons-related sites.

Other governments have also voiced opinions regarding the security of Pakistan's nuclear arsenal. For example, Indian National Security Adviser M. K. Narayanan said that the arsenal is safe and has adequate checks and balances.[119] Similarly, then-Secretary of State for Foreign and Commonwealth Affairs David Miliband told the *Charlie Rose Show* December 15, 2008, that Islamabad's nuclear weapons "are under pretty close lock and key." Furthermore, according to Director of the French General Directorate of External Security Erard Corbin de Mangoux, Pakistan's military and civilian leaders have a "sense of responsibility" to maintain control over the country's nuclear weapons; these leaders "know that the international status to which they aspire depends directly on their ability to exercise complete control over such an instrument of power," he argued in an interview published in spring 2010.[120]

Other non-U.S. officials, however, have sounded somewhat less optimistic. For example, Russian Deputy Prime Minister Sergei Ivanov said in a March 24, 2009, television interview that Moscow is "very much concerned" about the security of Pakistan's arsenal.[121] Indian officials expressed

---

(...continued)

0,2933,519696,00 html.

[117] Secretary of Defense Robert Gates, "Express TV Interview," January 21, 2010.

[118] "Security and Stability in Pakistan: Developments in U.S. Policy And Funding," *Hearing of the House Armed Services Committee*, April 29, 2010.

[119] "Pak Nukes Safely Guarded, Says Narayanan," *The Press Trust of India*, December 16, 2007.

[120] Isabelle Lasserre, "Intelligence and the New Threats," *Politique Internationale*, January 1-March 31, 2010.

[121] Lyubov Pronina and Ellen Pinchuk, "Russia 'Concerned' About Security of Pakistan's Nuclear Arsenal," *Bloomberg*, March 25, 2009.

concerns about the security of Pakistan's nuclear arsenal following the May 2011 insurgent attack on the Karachi military installation.[122]

Pakistani officials have consistently expressed confidence in the security of the country's nuclear arsenal.[123] Then-President Musharraf stated in November 2007 that Pakistan's nuclear weapons are under "total custodial controls."[124] More recently, President Asif Ali Zardari told *CNN* December 2, 2008, that the country's nuclear command and control system "is working well." Additionally, a Pakistani Foreign Ministry spokesperson stated May 21, 2009, that "there is simply no question of our strategic assets falling into the wrong hands. We have full confidence in our procedures, mechanisms and command and control systems." Pakistani Prime Minister Yousaf Raza Gilani stated May 8, 2010, that Islamabad has "laid to rest" concerns about its nuclear arsenal's security.[125]

The May 2011 U.S. strike that killed Al Qaeda leader Osama bin Laden generated a public discussion in Pakistan as to whether a country such as India or the United States could successfully attack and destroy Pakistan's nuclear weapons.[126] Responding to these concerns, Prime Minster Gilani stated May 25, 2011, that the country's "strategic assets are well protected and our capability to defend our sovereignty, territorial integrity and liberties of our people, is very much in place."[127]

In addition to the above scenarios, the security of Pakistan's nuclear weapons could also be jeopardized by another conflict between India and Pakistan, Michael Krepon argued, explaining that an "escalating war with nuclear forces in the field would increase the probability of accidents, miscalculations, and the use of nuclear weapons." This is because

> [w]hen tensions rise precipitously with India, the readiness level of Pakistan's nuclear deterrent also rises. Because the geographical coordinates of Pakistan's main nuclear weapon storage sites, missile, and air bases can be readily identified from satellites—and therefore targeted by opposing forces—the dictates of deterrence mandate some movement of launchers and weapons from fixed locations during crises. Nuclear weapons on the move are inherently less secure than nuclear weapons at heavily-guarded storage sites. Weapons and launchers in motion are also more susceptible to "insider" threats and accidents.[128]

---

[122] "Safety of Pakistan's Nukes a Global Concern: India," *Indo-Asian News Service*, May 25, 2011.

[123] Air Commodore Khalid Banuri, Director of Arms Control and Disarmament Affairs in the SPD, stated in a 2008 interview that Islamabad has "consistently augmented" its nuclear weapons security since 1998 (Ahmed Quraishi, "Interview: Air Commodore Khalid Banuri – 'Don't Mess With Pakistan'," January 17, 2008), http://www.globalpolitician.com/24013-pakistan.

[124] "Pakistan Nukes Under Control: Musharraf," *Agence France Presse*, November 13, 2007.

[125] "Pakistan conducts successful launches Hatf III (Ghaznavi) and Hatf IV (Shaheen 1)," *Pakistan Official News*, May 8, 2010.

[126] Jane Perlez, "Pakistan Army Under Scrutiny After U.S. Raid," *New York Times*, May 5, 2011; Zahid Hussain, Matthew Rosenberg and Jeremy Page, "After Raid, Confused Response," *The Wall Street Journal*, May 9, 2011; Toby Dalton and George Perkovich, "Beware Decline in Pakistani Relations," *Politico*, May 16, 2011.

[127] Press Information Department, "Prime Minister Gilani's Opening Statement at the Defence Committee of the Cabinet," *Pakistan Official News*, May 25, 2011.

[128] Krepon, June 12, 2008.

Such a war, Krepon added, would also place stress on the army's unity of command. Krepon has also pointed out that Islamabad faces a dilemma, because less-dispersed nuclear weapons may be more vulnerable to a disarming military strike from India.[129]

U.S. Assistance and Pakistani Nuclear Security

U.S. plans to secure Pakistani nuclear weapons in case of a loss of control by the Pakistani government were famously addressed during former Secretary of State Condoleezza Rice's confirmation hearing in January 2005. In response to a question from Senator John Kerry asking what would happen to Pakistan's nuclear weapons in the event of a radical Islamic coup in Islamabad, Secretary Rice answered, "[w]e have noted this problem, and we are prepared to try to deal with it."[130] On November 12, 2007, responding to press reports about this contingency, a Pakistan Foreign Office spokesperson said, "Pakistan possesses adequate retaliatory capacity to defend its strategic assets and sovereignty," emphasizing that Islamabad's nuclear weapons have been under "strong multi-layered, institutionalized decision-making, organizational, administrative and command and control structures since 1998."[131] The issue of U.S. contingency plans to take over Pakistani strategic assets was raised again in the press following Benazir Bhutto's assassination, and was met with similar assurances by Pakistan's government.[132]

More recently, a Pakistan Foreign Office spokesperson, responding to a report detailing alleged U.S.-Pakistani discussions regarding contingency plans for U.S. forces to help secure Islamabad's nuclear weapons, stated November 8, 2009, that Pakistan "does not require any foreign assistance in this regard." Pakistan will never "allow any country to have direct or indirect access to its nuclear and strategic facilities," the spokesperson said, adding that "no talks have ever taken place on the issue of the security of Pakistan's nuclear arsenal with US officials."[133] U.S. Ambassador to Pakistan Anne Patterson stated the same day that the United States "has no intention to seize Pakistani nuclear weapons or material." Gates stated during the January 2010 television interview that the United States has "no intention or desire to take over any of Pakistan's nuclear weapons."[134]

The United States reportedly offered nuclear security assistance to Pakistan soon after September 11, 2001.[135] U.S. assistance to Islamabad, which must comply with nonproliferation guidelines, has reportedly included the sharing of best practices and technical measures to prevent unauthorized or accidental use of nuclear weapons, as well as contribute to physical security of

---

[129] Michael Krepon, "Complexities Of Nuclear Risk Reduction In South Asia," *The Hindu*, May 29, 2009.

[130] "The Nomination of Dr. Condoleezza Rice to be Secretary of State," Hearings before the Senate Foreign Relations Committee, January 18 and 19, 2005. The concept of a contingency plan to take over Pakistan's nuclear assets was first written about by Seymour Hersh, "Watching the Warheads," *The New Yorker*, November 5, 2001.

[131] "Strategic Assets Are Safe, Says FO," *Dawn*, November 12, 2007.

[132] "Pentagon Readies Plan for Pakistan's Nuclear Arsenal," *The Guardian*, December 28, 2007. For a discussion of the difficulties of such a scenario, see Shaun Gregory, "The Security of Nuclear Weapons in Pakistan," Pakistan Security Research Unit Brief Number 22, University of Bradford, November 18, 2007. Available at http://spaces.brad.ac.uk:8080/download/attachments/748/Brief_22finalised.pdf

[133] "Pakistan Foreign Office Rejects U.S. Media Report on Nuclear Arsenal," *Associated Press of Pakistan*, November 9, 2009.

[134] "Express TV Interview," January 21, 2010.

[135] Alex Wagner, "U.S. Offers Nuclear Security Assistance to Pakistan," *Arms Control Today*, December 2001. http://www.armscontrol.org/act/2001_12/paknucsecdec01.asp.

storage facilities and personnel reliability.[136] As noted above, Islamabad employs a system requiring that at least two, and perhaps three, people authenticate launch codes for nuclear weapons.[137] Security at nuclear sites in Islamabad is the responsibility of a 10,000-member security force, commanded by a two-star general. Former Pakistani military officials have said Pakistan has developed Permissive Action Links (PALs) for its warheads without U.S. assistance.[138] PALs require a code to be entered before a weapon can be detonated.

Former Deputy Secretary of State Richard Armitage confirmed in a November 2007 interview that there has been U.S. assistance in this area, explaining that the United States was unlikely to intervene militarily in a crisis in Pakistan because "we have spent considerable time with the Pakistani military, talking with them and working with them on the security of their nuclear weapons. I think most observers would say that they are fairly secure. They have pretty sophisticated mechanisms to guard the security of those."[139] Rolf Mowatt-Larssen, former Director of the Office of Intelligence and Counterintelligence at the U.S. Department of Energy, pointed out in May 2009 that "there's not a lot of transparency into" how Islamabad spends the U.S. funds, but he nevertheless characterized them as "money well spent."[140] A Pakistani official said in November 2009 that Pakistan reserves the right to "pick and choose" the nuclear security measures it will undertake, adding that Islamabad will only accept such measures that are "non-intrusive."[141]

The extent to which Pakistan has shared information about its nuclear arsenal with the United States is unclear. Although, as noted, former President Musharraf has acknowledged Islamabad's sharing of some information, General Tariq Majid, chair of Pakistan's Joint Chiefs of Staff Committee, stated November 9, 2009, that "there is absolutely no question of sharing or allowing any foreign individual, entity or a state, any access to sensitive information about our nuclear assets."[142] Air Commodore Khalid Banuri, Director of Arms Control and Disarmament Affairs in the SPD, indicated in a 2008 interview that Islamabad accepts U.S. "education and awareness, but in a completely non-intrusive way," adding that Pakistan has "some rudimentary equipment and some training" from the United States. Banuri described giving U.S. officials access to Pakistan's nuclear weapons facilities as a "red line" that Islamabad will not cross.[143]

The U.S. government has also reportedly offered assistance to secure or destroy radioactive materials that could be used to make a radioactive dispersal device, and to ship highly enriched uranium used in the Pakistani civilian nuclear sector out of the country.[144] Pakistan's response to

---

[136] Joby Warrick, "U.S. Has Concerns Over Security of Pakistan's Nuclear Weapons," *The Washington Post*, November 11, 2007; David Sanger and William Broad, "U.S. Secretly Aids Pakistan in Guarding Nuclear Arms," *The New York Times*, November 17, 2007.

[137] Mubarakmand provided some details about Pakistan's use of such codes in the 2004 interview.

[138] General Kidwai has stated that "if a country can make complex nuclear weapons and ballistic cruise missiles grant it that PALs is a far simpler technology" (cited in Martellini, 2008).

[139] "A Conversation With Former Deputy Secretary of State Richard Armitage," *PBS: The Charlie Rose Show*, November 6, 2007.

[140] Ben Arnoldy, "Could Taliban Get Keys to Pakistan's A-Bomb? Experts See the Islamic Fighters as Less of a Risk than Radical Insiders Gaining Access to Nuclear Materials," *The Christian Science Monitor*, May 15, 2009.

[141] Mariana Baabar, "Pak N-safety Plan," *The News International*, November 10, 2009.

[142] *Ibid.*

[143] Quraishi, January 17, 2008.

[144] Bryan Bender, "Pakistan, US in Talks on Nuclear Security," *The Boston Globe*, May 5, 2009.

---

these proposals is unclear, and downturns in the bilateral relationship overall may have complicated efforts to make progress in this area.

It is worth noting that, according to some observers, spent fuel from Pakistan's Karachi and Chasma nuclear power plants could be vulnerable to theft or attack.[145] However, Pakistani officials have expressed confidence in the security of its facilities[146] and have said that Islamabad has no plans to transport spent fuel from either reactor. Moreover, the Pakistan Nuclear Regulatory Authority (PNRA) has a Nuclear Security Action Plan, which includes a description of regulations for handling spent nuclear fuel. The PNRA states that Pakistan follows IAEA physical protection standards.[147]

Proliferation

A fundamental aspect of nuclear security is ensuring that personnel with sensitive knowledge do not proliferate that expertise, but this aspect of nuclear security in Pakistan was recognized only in the past 10 years and resulted in significant reforms of its personnel security system. Many observers continue to be concerned that other states or terrorist organizations could obtain material or expertise related to nuclear weapons from elements in Pakistan.[148] This view is only encouraged by recent instability and governance problems.

The A. Q. Khan Network

Proliferation networks stemming from Pakistan have their roots in the effort to develop a Pakistani nuclear bomb. Beginning in the 1970s, Pakistan used extensive clandestine procurement networks to obtain technology for its own nuclear weapons program. A report from Pakistan's Inter-Services Intelligence published September 15, 2011, stated that Pakistan, as an

> under-developed country with no industrial infra-structure, had to buy each and every bit of material and piece of equipment surreptitiously from abroad in the open market and had to establish a network of cover companies within the country and outside to by-pass embargoes and import all the necessary items.[149]

Former Pakistani nuclear scientist A. Q. Khan directed this procurement and subsequently used a similar network to supply Libya, North Korea, and Iran with designs and materials related to uranium enrichment for profit.[150] [151]

---

[145] Abdul Mannan, "Preventing Nuclear Terrorism in Pakistan: Sabotage of a Spent Fuel Cask or a Commercial Irradiation Source in Transport," in *Pakistan's Nuclear Future*, 2008; Martellini, 2008. More details about these facilities may be found in the section, "Pakistan's Civil Nuclear Program." Some analysts argue that spent nuclear fuel is more vulnerable when being transported.

[146] Martellini, 2008.

[147] These standards are contained in IAEA document INFCIRC/225/Rev.4.

[148] For more information on Pakistani proliferation, see CRS Report RL32745, *Pakistan's Nuclear Proliferation Activities and the Recommendations of the 9/11 Commission: U.S. Policy Constraints and Options*, by Richard P. Cronin, K. Alan Kronstadt, and Sharon Squassoni. Also see CRS Report RL33498, *Pakistan-U.S. Relations*, by K. Alan Kronstadt.

[149] Available at http://www.foxnews.com/world/2011/09/16/aq-khan-report-isi/#ixzz1Y9ZIgsQV.

[150] Libya obtained uranium enrichment technology and nuclear weapons designs that could support a nuclear weapons
(continued...)

The current status of Pakistan's nuclear export network is unclear, although most official U.S. reports indicate that, at the least, it has been damaged considerably. Then-Director of National Intelligence John D. Negroponte implied that the network had been dismantled when he asserted in a January 11, 2007, statement to the Senate Select Committee on Intelligence that "Pakistan had been a major source of nuclear proliferation until the disruption of the A. Q. Khan network."[152] When asked about the network's current status during a July 25, 2007, Senate Foreign Relations Committee hearing, then-Under Secretary for Political Affairs Nicholas Burns replied that

> I cannot assert that no part of that network exists, but it's my understanding based on our conversations with the Pakistanis that the network has been fundamentally dismantled. But to say that there are no elements in Pakistan, I'm not sure I could say that.

Similarly, the London-based International Institute for Strategic Studies found in a May 2007 report that "at least some of Khan's associates appear to have escaped law enforcement attention and could ... resume their black-market business."[153]

More recently, a January 12, 2009, State Department press release said that the network "is no longer operating." For its part, Pakistan's Foreign Office stated February 7, 2009, that Pakistan "has dismantled the nuclear black market network." Asked during a July 20, 2009, interview whether Pakistan was transferring "nuclear weapons" or related advice to North Korea, Secretary of State Hillary Clinton replied that there is "no evidence" that Pakistan is doing so. Furthermore, Acting Assistant Secretary of State Vann Van Diepen described the network as "basically defunct"

(...continued)

program. North Korea currently has a plutonium-based nuclear weapons program and may also have a uranium-based nuclear weapons program. Iran is suspected of pursuing both plutonium- and uranium-based nuclear weapons programs. Such activity has been of historic concern; a 1979 State Department memorandum stated that Libya, Iraq, or Iran "might be prepared to provide economic support" to Islamabad "in exchange for nuclear cooperation from Pakistan." (Department of State Action Memorandum, "PRC Paper on South Asia," March 23, 1979, available at http://www.gwu.edu/~nsarchiv/nukevault/ebb333/doc41.PDF). Additionally, a 1979 memorandum from the National Intelligence Officer for Nuclear Proliferation stated that Pakistan "might already have been induced to share with identified foreigners some sensitive nuclear equipment and to propose terms for possible future nuclear cooperation with Saudi Arabia, Libya, or Iraq." ("Monthly Warning Report – Nuclear Proliferation," NFAC – 3871-79, July 24, 1979, available at http://www.gwu.edu/~nsarchiv/nukevault/ebb333/doc32a.pdf).

[151] The network also supplied Libya with "documents related to the design and fabrication of a nuclear explosive device," according to the IAEA (*Implementation of the NPT Safeguards Agreement in the Socialist People's Libyan Arab Jamahiriya*, GOV/2008/39, September 12, 2008). However, these documents lacked "important parts" for making a nuclear weapon, according to former IAEA Director-General Mohamed ElBaradei (*The Age of Deception*: *Nuclear Diplomacy in Treacherous Times* (New York: Metropolitan Books), 2011, p. 155). Moreover, Khan told a former member of his network that he had "supplied the Libyans with plans for a non-working nuclear device" (*Extract from the Statement of Sayed Abu Tahir Bin Bukhary*, June 7, 2006, Annexure L in Plea and Sentence Agreement, State vs. Geiges, Wisser, and Krisch Engineering, September 2007). The International Institute for Strategic Studies described the design as "95% complete" (*Nuclear Black Markets*, 2007, p. 79).

In addition to the documents supplied to Tripoli, members of the network also had computer files containing "drawings for the components of two smaller, more advanced nuclear weapons" (David Albright, *Peddling Peril*: *How the Secret Nuclear Trade Arms America's Enemies*, The Institute for Science and International Security, 2010. p.151). However, according to former IAEA official Olli Heinonen, these "detailed designs" were not "complete sets" of weapons design information. Heinonen suggested that other members of the network could have possessed more complete nuclear weapons designs (interview with CRS analyst, August 4, 2011).

[152] Unclassified Statement for the Record Annual Threat Assessment, Senate Select Committee on Intelligence, January 11, 2007.

[153] *Nuclear Black Markets*, 2007, p. 159.

---

during a July 22, 2010, congressional hearing, adding that "we're on the lookout for sort of the next A.Q. Khan network, so to speak."[154] Similarly, State Department spokesperson P.J. Crowley told reporters during an August 3, 2010, press briefing that the United States monitors the Khan network "very closely for signs that others within his realm are still in business." A March 2012 State Department report described the network as "defunct."[155]

Asked during the 2007 hearing about Pakistan's cooperation in investigating the network, Burns acknowledged that the United States has not had "personal, consistent access" to Khan, but added that he did not "have all the details of everything we've done." Similarly, the IAEA has not yet been able to interview Khan directly, according to an agency official. However, sources report that Islamabad has responded to written questions from the IAEA and has been cooperative with the agency's investigation of Iran's nuclear program.[156] Former IAEA official Olli Heinonen, who investigated the Khan network during his time at the agency, stated in an interview published in October 2011 that Khan "answer[ed] some of my questions in writing through secret channels."[157] Khan himself told *Dawn News TV* May 29, 2008, that he would not cooperate with U.S. or IAEA investigators. A Pakistani Foreign Office spokesperson told reporters in May 2006 that the government considered the Khan investigation "closed"—a position an office spokesperson reiterated February 6, 2009. The State Department announced January 12, 2009, that it was imposing sanctions on 13 individuals and three companies for their involvement in the Khan network. The sanctions were imposed under the Export-Import Bank Act, the Nuclear Proliferation Prevention Act, and Executive Orders 12938 and 13382. Pursuant to a requirement in the Enhanced Partnership with Pakistan Act of 2009 (P.L. 111-73), Secretary of State Hillary Clinton issued a certification on March 18, 2011, that Pakistan "is continuing to cooperate with the United States in efforts to dismantle supplier networks relating to the acquisition of nuclear weapons-related materials."

Interactions with Al-Qaeda

According to reports, Al-Qaeda unsuccessfully sought nuclear weapons assistance from the Khan network[158] but did receive limited help from at least one other group in Pakistan. Scientists who may have provided some help to al-Qaeda representatives were retired Pakistan Atomic Energy Commission scientists, long-time rivals of A. Q. Khan, and Islamic fundamentalists—Sultan Bashiruddin Mahmood and Chaudiri Abdul Majeed.[159] The assistance under the umbrella of the UTN humanitarian organization was reportedly related to weapons of mass destruction, but details are scarce on the extent of the transfers, and the events following the September 11, 2001, attacks on the United States may have cut off this interaction.

---

[154] "Transshipment And Diversion: Are U.S. Trading Partners Doing Enough To Prevent The Spread Of Dangerous Technologies?" *Hearing of the Terrorism, Nonproliferation and Trade Subcommittee of the House Foreign Affairs Committee*, July 22, 2010.

[155] *Report To Congress: Update on Progress toward Regional Nuclear Nonproliferation in South Asia*, submitted March 20, 2012.

[156] Personal communication, November 9, 2007.

[157] "Former IAEA Deputy Chief Voices Concern About Iran, North Korea, Pakistan," *Der Spiegel*, October 2, 2011.

[158] Former Director of Central Intelligence George Tenet wrote in his memoirs that the United States "received fragmentary information from an intelligence service" that in 1998 Osama bin Laden had "sent emissaries to establish contact" with the Khan network. Tenet, George and Harlow, Bill, *At the Center of the Storm: My Years at the CIA*, HarperCollins: New York, 2007. p. 261; Albright, *Peddling Peril*, 2010.

[159] For a detailed discussion, see Albright, 2010.

Mahmood and Majeed met with Osama bin Laden and Ayman al-Zawahiri in August 2001 in Afghanistan to discuss, among other topics, what would be needed to develop a nuclear weapons infrastructure, details of nuclear bomb design, and how to construct radiological dispersal devices.[160] Mahmood was a public figure well-known for his eccentric and extreme views about science and Islam, and he was demoted in 1999 to a lower rank in part because of his radicalism. Mahmood then sought early retirement and started the UTN organization. After the United States briefed the Pakistani government about this activity at the highest levels in the fall of 2001, the Pakistani authorities detained the UTN scientists for multiple rounds of questioning. Through these interrogations and searches in Afghanistan, UTN's work with al-Qaeda on biological weapons and rudimentary nuclear weapons technology came to light.[161] The Pakistani government did not press criminal charges against Mahmood and Majeed, but put the scientists under house arrest in 2002. This extreme case raised awareness of the "insider threat" and subsequently led to changes in Pakistani personnel security policy, detailed below. Accounts raise the possibility of other groups or individuals also providing al Qaeda with nuclear expertise, but less information is publicly available.[162]

Pakistan's Response to the Proliferation Threat

Then-Under Secretary Burns testified in July 2007 that the Bush Administration has "told the Pakistani government that it is its responsibility ... to make sure" that neither the Khan network nor a "similar organization" resurfaces in the country. Since the revelations about the Khan network, Pakistan appears to have increased its efforts to prevent nuclear proliferation. But whether and to what extent these efforts have been successful is not yet clear. It is worth noting that, because Khan conducted his proliferation activities as a government official, they do not necessarily indicate a failure of Islamabad's export controls.

Pakistani officials argue that Islamabad has taken a number of steps to prevent further proliferation of nuclear-related technologies and materials.[163] For example, Islamabad adopted in September 2004 new national export controls legislation which includes a requirement that the government issue control lists for "goods, technologies, material, and equipment which may contribute to designing, development, stockpiling, [and] use" of nuclear weapons and related delivery systems. According to a February 2008 presentation by Zafar Ali, Director of Pakistan's Strategic Export Controls Division (SECDIV),[164] the lists, which were issued in October 2005 and are to be periodically updated, include items controlled by multilateral export control regimes, such as the Nuclear Suppliers Group, the Australia Group, and the Missile Technology Control Regime.[165] The export controls legislation also includes a catch-all clause, which requires

---

[160] Albright, ibid. According to a 2005 report by the Commission on the Intelligence Capabilities of the United States Regarding Weapons of Mass Destruction, al-Qaeda "had established contact with Pakistani scientists who discussed development of nuclear devices that would require hard-to-obtain materials like uranium to create a nuclear explosion. http://www.wmd.gov/report/index.html.

[161] Albright, ibid. Tenet, ibid.

[162] Albright, ibid.

[163] Details of Pakistan's nuclear-related legislation can be found in the country's reports to the UN 1540 Committee. Both can be found at http://daccessdds.un.org/doc/UNDOC/GEN/N04/597/46/PDF/N0459746.pdf?OpenElement.

[164] Presentation given to Partnership for Global Security Workshop, "Meeting the Nuclear Security Challenge in Pakistan," February 21-22, 2008. http://www.partnershipforglobalsecurity.org/documents/zafar_export.pdf.

[165] The Nuclear Suppliers Group is a multilateral, voluntary group of nuclear supplier states which have agreed to coordinate their exports of civilian nuclear technology and materials in order to prevent importers from using them to (continued...)

---

exporters to notify the government if they are aware or suspect that goods or technology are intended by the end-user for use in nuclear or biological weapons, or missiles capable of delivering such weapons.[166]

The legislation includes several other important elements, such as end-use and end-user certification requirements and new penalties for violators. Since its adoption, Pakistan has established the SECDIV and an associated Oversight Board. The SECDIV is responsible for formulating rules and regulations for implementing the legislation. The board is comprised of officials from multiple agencies and is headed by Pakistan's Foreign Secretary.

Islamabad says that it has also taken several other steps to improve its nuclear security. For example, the government announced in June 2007 that it is "implementing a National Security Action Plan with the [IAEA's] assistance." That same month, Pakistan also joined the U.S.- and Russian-led Global Initiative to Combat Nuclear Terrorism. As noted above, the December 2007 National Command Authority Ordinance also includes measures to prevent the spread of nuclear-related materials and expertise.

Pakistani officials participating in an April 2007 Partnership for Global Security workshop argued that Islamabad has improved the reliability of its nuclear personnel by, for example, making security clearance procedures more stringent. However, the officials also acknowledged that Islamabad still needs to do more to control its nuclear expertise.[167] Similarly, Admiral Mullen stated May 14, 2009, that the country's personnel reliability system must "continue to improve." Some reports about the early January 2011 shooting of Salmaan Taseer, the governor of Punjab province, have raised questions about Pakistan's ability to vet security personnel properly.[168]

The United States has also provided export control assistance to Pakistan. Burns described several such efforts in his July 2007 testimony.[169] And according to an October 2007 U.S. Government Accountability Office report, Islamabad was during FY2003-FY2006 the second-largest recipient

---

(...continued)

produce nuclear weapons. The Australia Group is a voluntary, informal, export-control arrangement through which participating countries coordinate their national export controls to limit the supply of chemicals and biological agents, as well as related equipment, technologies, and knowledge, to countries and nonstate entities suspected of pursuing chemical or biological weapons capabilities. The Missile Technology Control Regime is an informal, voluntary arrangement in which participants agree to adhere to common export policy guidelines applied to an "annex" that lists items related to the proliferation of ballistic and cruise missiles, rockets, and unmanned air vehicles capable of delivering weapons of mass destruction.

[166] The Chemical Weapons Convention Implementation Ordinance of 2000 regulates the import and export of chemicals in accordance with the convention.

[167] Building Confidence in Pakistan's Nuclear Security: Workshop Synopsis. April 30, 2007.

[168] Asif Shahzad, "Pakistani Governor Killed by own Bodyguard," *Associated Press*, January 4, 2011; Salman Masood and Carlotta Gall, "Crisis Grows in Pakistan with Killing of Governor; Government Shaken amid Fears Islamists have Infiltrated Security Forces," *The International Herald Tribune*, January 6, 2011; Asif Shahzad and Sebastian Abbot, "Shadow over Pakistan Security Grows," *Associated Press*, January 12, 2011.

[169] Burns mentioned Pakistan's participation in the Container Security Initiative and the Secure Freight Initiative. Under these programs, "the United States and Pakistan worked together to install screening and radiation detection equipment to scan U.S.-bound cargo." He also stated that the Department of Energy "is working with Pakistan on radiation source security and is in the process of finalizing an agreement to install radiation detection equipment at Pakistani ports and border crossings."

---

of bilateral U.S. assistance designed to improve target countries' export controls. Pakistan received such assistance from the Departments of State, Energy, and Homeland Security.[170]

Under Secretary of State for Arms Control and International Security Ellen Tauscher told the Senate Foreign Relations Committee that the Obama Administration does not support conditioning aid to Pakistan on permitting direct U.S. access to Khan, arguing, in part, that the United States has "obtained a great deal of information about the Khan network without having direct access to A.Q. Khan."[171]

Pakistan's Civil Nuclear Program

Pakistan also has a civil nuclear power program, with two reactors currently operating—the Karachi Nuclear Power Plant, which went critical in 1971,[172] and the Chasma Nuclear Power Plant, which went critical in 2000.[173] Prime Minister Gilani announced May 12, 2011, that a second nuclear reactor at Chasma, constructed with Chinese assistance, had become operational.[174] Beijing has also apparently agreed to construct two additional power reactors at Chasma, according to both Chinese and Pakistani officials.[175] Pakistan Atomic Energy Commission Chairman Ansar Parvez stated May 12, 2011, that concrete has been poured for one of these reactors and that ground breaking for the other reactor would take place the next month. The first reactor is to come on line in 2016, with the next to follow 10 months later.[176] Acting Assistant Secretary Van Diepen stated July 22, 2010, that such a sale would appear to be inconsistent with current Nuclear Suppliers Group (NSG) guidelines. Additionally, Pakistan and China are reportedly close to finalizing an agreement for Beijing to construct a third, larger, reactor in Pakistan.[177] As noted, the NSG changed its guidelines in 2008 to allow nuclear trade with India. Secretary of State Clinton suggested July 20, 2010, that the United States does not currently support a similar change for Pakistan.[178] Assistant Secretary of State Robert Blake reiterated Van Diepen and Clinton's positions March 18, 2011.[179]

---

[170] GAO Report, *Nonproliferation: U.S. Efforts to Combat Nuclear Networks Need Better Data on Proliferation Risks and Program Results,* October 31, 2007.

[171] Question #54, Pre-Hearing Questions for the Record by Senator Richard Lugar Senate Foreign Relations Committee, Nomination of Ellen M. Tauscher to be Under Secretary of State for Arms Control and International Security. http://lugar.senate.gov/sfrc/pdf/TauscherQFR.pdf.

[172] http://www.paec.gov.pk/kanupp/ma htm.

[173] http://www.paec.gov.pk/chasnupp1/milestones htm.

[174] Shafek E Koreshe, "Pakistan's Third 330 MW Nuclear Power Plant Becomes Operational," *Associated Press of Pakistan*, May 12, 2011.

[175] *Ibid.*, Foreign Ministry Spokesman's News Conference on September 21, 2010. http://www mfa.gov.cn/eng/xwfw/s2510/2511/t756092 htm.

[176] Koreshe, 2011.

[177] "Pak's One-GW Nuke Plant Project Likely to be Finalised during Jiabao's Visit," *Asian News International,* December 7, 2010. Christopher Bodeen, "China's Wen to Visit India Amid Trade, Land Spats," *Associated Press*, December 12, 2010. Khurram Shahzad, "China, Pakistan Sign $20 Bln Deals: Minister," *Agence France Presse*, December 17, 2010.

[178] "Remarks by Secretary of State Hillary Rodham Clinton at a Town Hall at the Pakistan National Council of the Arts," July 20, 2010.

[179] Media Roundtable with Robert O. Blake, Jr., Assistant Secretary of State for South and Central Asian Affairs, March 18, 2011.

Pakistan is also operating two research reactors—Pakistan Research Reactor 1, which went critical in 1965,[180] and Pakistan Research Reactor 2, which went critical in 1989.[181] Pakistan Research Reactor 1, which was originally supplied by a U.S. firm, was converted from using highly-enriched uranium (HEU) to low-enriched uranium fuel in 1992.[182] A "small amount" of the HEU fuel remains in Pakistan.[183]

Issues for Congress

Legislation introduced during the 111th Congress appeared designed to influence Islamabad's nuclear stability and policies regarding the Khan network. Section 2 of H.R. 1463, which was introduced March 12, 2009, stated that U.S. military assistance could be provided to Pakistan only if the President were to certify that Islamabad is both making A. Q. Khan available to the United States for questioning and "providing adequate assurances to the United States Government that it will monitor Khan's movements and activities in such a manner as to prevent his participation in any efforts to disseminate nuclear technology or know-how." This section would have allowed the President to waive restrictions on U.S. assistance imposed pursuant to the proposed legislation if the President were to certify to Congress "that it is in the national interests of the United States to do so."

H.R. 2481, the United States-Pakistan Security and Stability Act, which was introduced May 19, 2009, would have required the President to "develop and transmit to the appropriate congressional committees a comprehensive interagency strategy and implementation plan for long-term security and stability in Pakistan." The strategy was to include a "description of how United States assistance" authorized by the bill would be "used to achieve the objectives of United States policy toward Pakistan," including enabling Islamabad to "maintain robust command and control over its nuclear weapons technology." The bill would have authorized foreign assistance for Pakistan, including funds for improving the government's counter-insurgency capability.

In addition, legislation to authorize various forms of U.S. assistance to Pakistan contains provisions related to Islamabad's nuclear program. S. 1707, the Enhanced Partnership with Pakistan Act of 2009, which became law (P.L. 111-73, 123 Stat. 2060) on October 15, 2009, authorizes various forms of U.S. assistance to Pakistan, including strengthening democratic institutions and law enforcement, as well as supporting economic development, education, human rights, and heath care. Section 203 (c) of S. 1707 requires the President to certify that Pakistan is "continuing to cooperate with the United States in efforts to dismantle supplier networks relating to the acquisition of nuclear weapons-related materials, such as providing relevant information from or direct access to Pakistani nationals associated with such networks." It also requires a Semi-Annual Monitoring Report that is to include a detailed description of Pakistan's nuclear non-proliferation efforts and an assessment of whether assistance has

---

[180] Research Reactor Details - PARR-1. http://www.iaea.org/worldatom/rrdb/.

[181] Research Reactor Details - PARR-2. http://www.iaea.org/worldatom/rrdb/.

[182] I.H. Qureshi, "Recollections From The Early Days Of The PAEC," *The Nucleus*, 42 (1-2), 2005, pp. 7-11. Research Reactor Details - PARR-1.

[183] Matthew Bunn, *Securing the Bomb 2010: Securing All Nuclear Materials in Four Years*, (Cambridge, MA., and Washington, DC: Project on Managing the Atom, Harvard University, and Nuclear Threat Initiative), April 2010, p. 28.

directly or indirectly aided the expansion of Pakistan's nuclear weapons program, whether by the diversion of United States assistance or the reallocation of Pakistan's financial resources that would otherwise be spent for programs and activities unrelated to its nuclear weapons program.

In response to concerns expressed in Pakistan over the intent of the bill, a "Joint Explanatory Statement" was submitted for the *Congressional Record* by Senate Foreign Relations Committee Chairman John Kerry and then-House Foreign Affairs Committee Chairman Howard Berman. The statement emphasizes that "the legislation does not seek in any way to compromise Pakistan's sovereignty, impinge on Pakistan's national security interests, or micromanage any aspect of Pakistani military or civilian operations." Regarding reporting requirements on nuclear nonproliferation cooperation, the statement says:

> The many requirements of this report are intended as a way for Congress to assess how effectively U.S. funds are being spent, shortfalls in U.S. resources that hinder the use of such funds, and steps the Government of Pakistan has taken to advance our mutual interests in countering extremism and nuclear proliferation and strengthening democratic institutions.

> There is no intent to, and nothing in this Act in any way suggests that there should be, any U.S. role in micromanaging internal Pakistani affairs, including the promotion of Pakistani military officers or the internal operations of the Pakistani military.[184]

S. 1707 represented a compromise between two bills, H.R. 1886, the Pakistan Enduring Assistance and Cooperation Enhancement Act of 2009, and S. 962, the Enhanced Partnership with Pakistan Act of 2009. H.R. 1886 would have placed conditions on U.S. security assistance to Pakistan; it stated that no U.S. military assistance could be provided to Pakistan if the President had not made a series of determinations, one of which is that the government "is continuing to cooperate with the United States in efforts to dismantle supplier networks relating to the acquisition of nuclear weapons related materials, including, as necessary, providing access to Pakistani nationals associated with such networks." The section included a national security waiver. The bill also required a report to Congress which would have included a "description of Pakistan's efforts to prevent proliferation of nuclear-related material and expertise" and an "assessment of whether assistance provided to Pakistan pursuant to this Act has directly or indirectly aided the expansion of Pakistan's nuclear weapons program." The committee report underlined ongoing concerns about getting full information about the activities of the Khan network and development of Pakistan's own nuclear arsenal:

> Pakistan's history of nuclear development and Dr. Abdul Qadeer Khan's establishment of a nuclear proliferation network remain a source for concern to many in the United States, particularly since the Committee understands that representatives of the United States have not interviewed certain individuals involved in the network. The Committee believes the United States should continue to engage the Government of Pakistan on the network, and should, as necessary, obtain direct access to the individuals covered by this subsection, including Dr. Khan. The Committee also maintains strong concerns regarding recent reports of Pakistan expansion of its nuclear arsenal. Given the expanding threat of Pakistan's domestic insurgency, the Government of Pakistan's further development of nuclear materials appears inconsistent with its immediate security threats and is unhelpful in the context of efforts to strengthen U.S.-Pakistani relations.

---

[184] See *Congressional Record* S10429-S10431.

S. 962 would have provided aid to Pakistan but did not include conditions regarding the nuclear nonproliferation or nuclear weapons activities. The Senate report (S.Rept. 111-33), however, stated that "[a]ny use of funds contained in this legislation for the purpose of augmenting Pakistan's nuclear weapons program would be directly contrary to Congressional intent."

It is worth noting that Pakistani officials have expressed interest in concluding a nuclear cooperation agreement with the United States, which would require congressional approval. Prime Minister Gilani told a visiting congressional delegation in June 2011 that such cooperation "would help build a positive image of the U.S. in the country."[185]

Author Contact Information

Paul K. Kerr
Analyst in Nonproliferation
pkerr@crs.loc.gov, 7-8693

Mary Beth Nikitin
Specialist in Nonproliferation
mnikitin@crs.loc.gov, 7-7745

---

[185] Press Information Department, "United States Congressional Delegation calls on Prime Minister Gilani," *Pakistan Official News*, June 7, 2011.